YOU SHOULD
SIT DOWN FOR THIS

YOU SHOULD SIT DOWN FOR THIS

A Memoir about Wine, Life, and Cookies

TAMERA MOWRY-HOUSLEY

LEGACY
LIT

BOSTON   NEW YORK

Legacy Lit, an imprint of Grand Central Publishing

Hachette Book Group
1290 Avenue of the Americas
New York, NY 10104
LegacyLitBooks.com
Twitter.com/LegacyLitBooks
Instagram.com/LegacyLitBooks

First Edition: October 2022

Grand Central Publishing is a division of Hachette Book Group, Inc. The Legacy Lit and Grand Central Publishing names and logos are trademarks of Hachette Book Group, Inc.

The Hachette Speakers Bureau provides a wide range of authors for speaking events.

To find out more, go to www.hachettespeakersbureau.com or call (866) 376-6591.

The publisher is not responsible for websites (or their content) that are not owned by the publisher.

Library of Congress Control Number: 2022939597

ISBNS: 978-0-3069-2595-5 (hardcover); 978-1-5387-4008-8 (signed edition); 978-1-5387-4009-5 (B&N signed edition); 978-0-3069-2596-2 (ebook)

Printed in the United States of America

LSC-C

Printing 1, 2022

I dedicate this book to the loves of my life that I lost three years ago that have changed my life forever.

Cloretha Richardson, my amazing grandmother. Your prayers and words of wisdom are still embedded in my soul and branded on my heart. You taught me everything I know about unconditional love and Godly joy. As you always say, there's a difference. Love you now and forever.

Alaina Maria Housley, how I miss you: your smile, your laughter, your phone calls. I could go on and on. As you know, I can be loquacious. I promise to tell my children and keep your memory alive. You touched my life deeply. Your kindness is something I will never forget. Auntie loves you. Till we meet again.

Conversation and High Tea

From the dictionary of Tamera Mowry-Housley

TAMERAISM:

A bite-size drop of wisdom that can spark happiness, inspire change, and empower you to live your most delicious life.

If you were to see me on the street, you might think, *Didn't I see you in* A Christmas Miracle? Or maybe, *I used to watch you on* Sister, Sister! *Wait, you were in* Twitches, *right? Which twitch are you, by the way??* Well, please know that I'll be happy to talk about all of that! Also know that I'll enjoy our conversation whether we talk about wine, shoes, Christmas, dogs, how old your kids are, or what it was like to work with comedic legends Jackée and Tim Reid. But sitting here, getting ready to write about my life feels different from a chance encounter. Putting the bulk of my life (so far!) down on paper is intimidating. Where does a girl even begin? Would anyone care that I was born two minutes before my sister, making me the older twin? How do I decide which stories to tell? How many tales can I tell from my life as a teen sitcom star in the '90s before things get dull? There is only so much one can say about bucket hats! This process is new to me, and there's no script to follow. There's no director giving me guidance about what works and what doesn't. I'm not doing a scene with another person—there's no back-and-forth to draw energy from. What I have in front of me is this blank page and forty-plus years of memories. Talk about intense! Can I remember the most important bits? Can I tell these stories well enough to do my life and everyone in it justice?

So, before I get into all this, I'm going to imagine that you are here with me. Let's just go ahead and make it a picture-perfect Napa Valley day. Can we just decide it's spring? It's warm but not hot, and the sun is bright and cheering. I open the door to let you in, and I greet you with a big hug. (I'm a hugger.) I'm wearing a breezy blue summer dress, and we banter a bit about the glory of spring—the world is in bloom! *Did you see the lilacs?* I lead you through the hallway, which is lined with family photographs, and into the kitchen. The late morning sunshine spills through the windows, lighting up everything. I'm glad I made sure the kitchen was spotless—no hiding anything on all these white surfaces in this bright light. The weather might be getting warmer, but I don't consider baking to be just a cold weather activity. *It smells good in here, right?* There is nothing as welcoming and comforting as the smell of butter, sugar, and chocolate. And isn't it perfect that you arrived just as I'm about to pull out the first batch? The timer dings, and I slip on an oven mitt. I pull my signature chocolate chips cookies out of the oven and onto a cooling rack that I've placed in the middle of the island—where we can both reach it easily. By the way, I've been known to polish off quite a few of these, so consider yourself warned. And I have a few other treats lined up for our afternoon together.

As I prepare the next batch to go in, I'll ask you how you take your coffee—or maybe you're a tea person? It doesn't matter. I am prepared to handle it all.

The cookies are in, the timer is set. I've brewed a pot of Earl Grey, set out my prettiest teacups, and pushed containers of sugar and cream in your direction. *Go ahead— please don't wait for me. Know I am willing to share my recipe if you want it. Please—sit down and get comfortable.* Because I'm going to tell you a story about a little Black girl who had big dreams and grand ambitions. She failed plenty, enjoyed many successes, doubted herself, almost quit, shed tears, cried a ton, but learned how to laugh some more through it all. Or at least find the grace in both the highs and lows.

I've certainly had my share of ups and downs, but through the heartache and laughter there were some simple constants that kept me going—dozens of chocolate chip cookies, beautiful glasses of red wine, and a fair amount of cleaning. Now I love baking, but truth be told I'm drawn to the simpler, more classic desserts. We've covered cookies, but I'm also partial to a warm slice of apple pie or a piece of perfect banana bread—preferably studded with dark chocolate chips. Satisfying and delicious, and I think they're the ideal treats to offer a friend while you're just hanging out and having a chat. Then there are those bigger, deeper conversations about the intricacies of life that are best served alongside a little treat with a special ingredient. The special ingredient that adds an extra pop of flavor are my Tameraisms.

Tameraisms are gorgeous bite-size drops of wisdom that have the power to enlighten us, keep us grounded, and occasionally rock us to our core. Tameraisms pack a powerful enough punch to make you think, *Whoa, that was something*, but they aren't going to leave you groggy from too much sweetness either. These little decked-out pockets of truth have been a guiding factor for me, and they've inspired each of the stories I'm going to share with you in these pages.

Please sit back and relax! And I hope you brought your

appetite because I plan to keep the treats coming, both savory and sweet. The petits fours, mini cheesecakes, tiny lemon tarts, and some mini chocolate tea cakes will be served up soon enough. There's no need for either of us to be polite: I expect you to eat up. I can easily brew another pot of tea and I can bake until the cows come home. This is my story, and I'm just glad you're with me, willing to hear it.

THE PAST

This course opens with a beauty pageant

followed by a delectable performance

at a local mall. Next, we'll move to

Los Angeles, where we will enjoy one of

my house specialties, layers of failure

topped off with a sprinkle of massive

success.

Chapter One

Mini-Queens and Silkworms

Here's a question (admittedly a weird one): If you were a fabric, which one would you be? A classic but crisp cotton that's as light as a breath of fresh air? Or maybe you're more like a durable, dependable polyblend that won't succumb to wrinkles *no matter what*. An ultrarich cashmere as comfortable as a hug is always beloved. Or maybe you're wool—naturally warm but with a touch of roughness. As for me, I'd want to be silk—smooth but never slippery, light and cool and wonderfully soft. And oddly enough, I once got to be silk in a local play.

WELCOME TO THE COPPERA'S COVE,
COMMUNITY PRODUCTION OF...
Textiles of the World

The nervousness I felt while waiting to go on stage was *intense*. I was one of the only kids cast in the production. The butterflies in my stomach were as big as birds, my palms were slick with sweat, and I was worried the audience would see my knees shaking. The other cast members played cotton, wool, and rayon, but I had been cast as silk. Silk! The fabric used for fancy dresses and wedding gowns. So elegant, I thought! Yes, I am silk inside and out!

I was determined to give this role my all. A friend of my mother's friend had kindly volunteered to make my costume—it was like a long, flowy apron. It would be a miracle if I didn't trip over it. My family and I had only lived in Texas for a short while, and I wasn't keen to be *that new Black girl, in a predominately white school, who fell on her face during the Textiles of the World play.* When the guy playing "polyester blend" finished his line, I took a big breath, gathered up my costume and walked onto a stage for the first time in my life. When the stage lights hit my face all the fear evaporated, revealing my inner mini-queen, who was ready to take charge. When I hit center stage I posed dramatically, stretching out my silk apron like it was a decadent work of art. I threw the audience a megawatt smile that I'm pretty sure I was born with. (Alas, I have no pictures to prove this. You'll just have to trust me.)

Then I delivered *the one line* that sparked my career,

which has spanned several decades. And what was the line that started it all—that line I delivered *with aplomb*? Here it goes...

Silk is a strong, lustrous fiber produced by silkworms.

cele

Picture me now, just a little bit older. The girl who played silk is now decked out in a miniature sailor suit. My red-and-white striped shirt shows just a hint of my bare waistline, and it's paired with a white skirt and is topped off with a jaunty little white sailor hat and the pièce de resistance... a fake telescope. *I'm a sailor—I must see far into the horizon!* I'm standing backstage in my first beauty pageant, watching Contestant Number Thirteen, who was on right before me. Number Thirteen was super fringed out in her ultrapink cowgirl apparel, when the emcee announced, "Next, we have one of our favorite champions! Let's give a warm welcome to contestant Number Thirteen!" Feeling nervous, I start feeding myself some positive self-talk: *Tamera, you are silk! Tamera, you are smooth and cooooool! Tamera, use your telescope to see into a future where you are a first place winner!!* Then I witnessed something magical. Thirteen didn't walk so much as glide/strut. She topped it all off with a side of bounce. Thirteen approached the judges' table and tossed her head gently, her picture perfect barrel curls remaining perfectly still thanks to a heavy dose of Aqua Net. She flashed a wide-eyed smile, her eyes and lips perfectly outlined—her makeup was *on point*. I thought about my fresh-and-nearly-make-up-free-face—I was thrilled that Mom let me put on a touch of mascara and a little bit of blush. Mom was a big believer in natural beauty, and based on the faces I was seeing around here she was definitely in the minority. Thirteen executed a slow turn, her fringe rippling into the wind behind her. She curtsied like an heir to the British throne and floated off the stage like a dream. I wanted TO DIE. I didn't want to lose the grand title to Little Miss Perfect.

The audience started clapping like mad. Thirteen waved cheerfully, skipping off the stage to a chorus of "ooohs" and "ahhhs" and "Isn't she just the sweetest thing?"

"Always a treat to see the gorgeous Number Thirteen!" said the emcee. How was I supposed to follow that? I had experienced Number Thirteen *types* before. They were everywhere. Sometimes it felt like Thirteens ruled the world—they were there when you turned on the TV— in commercials, sitcoms, and movies. A Number Thirteen was usually the most popular girl in her class, too, her perfection setting a high bar of prettiness and coolness for everyone else. And this girl, she was like the PROTOTYPE for Number Thirteen. I didn't see the likes of me anywhere in this competition. I had worked hard and I gotta say I looked cute, but what chance did I have in my homemade costume when those other girls looked like they were going to the Oscars? I knew I had talent, but how could I compete with kids whose parents hired professional choreographers and coaches? I knew the judges wouldn't take me seriously and there was no way I'd win. I wasn't a Number Thirteen. It probably didn't help that I was mixed race, with darker skin and natural, curly hair. I was being compared to the most perfect Number Thirteen of all time. I didn't fit the description of what a child beauty queen looked like. It was the over the top, ultra-polished pros they wanted. Not me.

The parade of sameness continued. During the talent competition one girl after another smiled widely while twirling Hula-Hoops, tossing batons, or executing a string of cartwheels. The environment of a beauty pageant is crazy. There is more makeup lying around than in a Sephora, as much behind-the-scenes drama as in an episode of *The Real Housewives*, and some of those girls had a laser-like focus to win. While there were the alpha Thirteens, there were also beta Number Thirteens. These girls were not as sharp and polished, but they were just as fierce in their determination to win—one effortlessly slid into splits in front of the judges' table with her little arms raised in triumph, holding her sparkly baton. These competitors came with tons of glittery, shimmery swag. If you've seen even five minutes of TLC's *Toddlers & Tiaras* you know what I'm talking about. Lastly, there was the category of girls (the one I fit into) which I'll refer to simply as *pageant-curious*. The pageant-curious group stayed away from a lot of the nonsense. They were girls who were there to hone their talent and/or their confidence.

So, picture me as that young mini-queen, no blinged-out Hula-Hoop, no big tricks, and definitely not sporting the looks of the typical Number Thirteen. I already stood out because of the color of my skin and natural curls, and my lack of a designer gown or face full of makeup made me feel even more out of my element. I just had my voice. Singing had always been my thing. I'd belt out Whitney Houston during all of our family car trips, and since as a military family we drove a lot of miles, these turned into hours-long solo concerts. I'd sing everywhere I went. I was a singing machine. I sang alone in my room or with my sister there sleeping, in the bathroom while showering, and even while brushing my teeth. Walking through a parking lot? I'd sing. I got to sing in church every Sunday, sandwiched in a pew between my parents and siblings, all of us dressed up in our "good clothes." Tia and I in pressed dresses and patent leather shoes, our brothers in button-down shirts and slightly crooked ties. When I sang in church, I'd feel the spirit wash over me. Nothing lifted me up like singing, and I was good at it.

As I stood on the stage, I realized (or felt since I was so young) that this was my chance to win. Even at that young age, I was beginning to understand that my voice was my secret weapon. I knew that I wasn't ever going be a Number Thirteen, but my voice could make up for everything else that I thought I wasn't at the time. My voice was my sparkle, my bling, bling. I walked onto the stage and stood in front of the microphone, which had been lowered to the right height for my size, aware that those big butterflies were back—and this time they were relentless.

The music started, and I let the opening line flow out of me...."I believe the children are our future." I had fallen head over heels in love with Whitney Houston. Whitney was a queen and I wanted to be just like her. I was enchanted by her beauty and elegance. One year for Christmas Tia and I each got walkmans that played cassette tapes. Tia was given the cassette of the album that was simply named *WHITNEY HOUSTON*, and on the cover she wore a dreamy peach evening gown and a single strand of pearls. I was so jealous! I wanted that Whitney Houston album, instead I got Stacey Q who was famous for her song Two of Hearts. Luckily, Tia let me borrow her Whitney cassette.

I continued to sing. The butterflies were gone now, my inner Whitney shining through. My shoulders dropped and my jaw relaxed, and I no longer cared about how different I was from the other contestants. I was killing this song, but then came the high note towards the end and just like that my voice cracked. It felt like my spirit broke in two along with it. I was crushed. I gave a bow while the audience clapped and cheered as heartily as they had for Number Thirteen. Standing alone on the stage, taking in the applause, I eyed the girls to my right behind the curtain. I knew I still stood out, but this time it was because my voice had the power to fill a room (even if I needed to work on those high notes).

Hours later, the pageant was nearly over. One shiny crown and three trophies had been placed on a table. We were finally going to find out who won.

I stood in a row of little girls in evening wear*—full-body sequin gowns in every color and sky-high hairdos. My natural hair, which usually seemed big, felt flat by comparison. The emcee walked over to the judges' table and was handed a clipboard (no thick cream-colored envelopes like the ones used at the Oscars). He walked back to the

---

*The notion of children in evening wear was ridiculous to me. Had any of us ever actually been up past 9 p.m.?

microphone, the audience clapping loudly. The level of excitement in the room was so high you'd think we were taking our final bow at the curtain call of a hit Broadway show. The buzz in the room increased as the judges announced the third runner-up. The girls all jumped up and down and smiled for their peers, the energy amping up all around me as we waited to learn who had placed in the talent portion of the competition. Suddenly the applause got louder, and I felt a gentle squeeze on my arm coming from the girl next to me. "Tamera! You won third runner-up. They just said your name!"

I was pushed gently forward, and I walked over to the emcee. The tiara for the third place winner of the talent competition wasn't as big as the Eiffel Tower of a crown the winner of the grand title would get, but it was more than enough for me. The tiara was plopped on my head, resting high and slightly crooked on top of my curly hair. A sash was placed over my shoulder, and I was handed a trophy that was nearly half my size. I took a little bow in front of the audience, waving happily, but I was surprised I had won. I also didn't understand why I wasn't happier about it. That all-consuming joy I felt when I played a silly piece of fabric was nonexistent. Why was this so different?

After the show my mom used Noxzema to remove

the makeup off of my face. The scent stung my eyes. She noticed I was unusually quiet. "What's the matter. Tamera? You did such a good job. You sang beautifully! Aren't you happy you won a trophy?" I didn't want to sound ungrateful, as I knew this experience took up two of my mother's most valuable resources: time and money. "What is it, Tamera? You can tell me," she begged to know.

"I know I won today, but I don't feel comfortable. This just isn't for me! I don't feel like I fit in. I'm not interested in putting all my energy into this—the fancy costumes, the professional make-up and hair, it's too much. I knew even then that the ultra-glitzy pageant world would never light up my soul.

I didn't know then that those feelings would follow me to Hollywood and into what would be considered a successful career. My mom nodded. She understood me.

"First things first. You ready to go to Dairy Queen?" I cheered up instantly at the thought of a chocolate dip ice cream cone. "Then Let's take this trophy home, and Tamera we'll look for something else for you. We'll figure it out. Get your stuff, and let's go."

TAMERAISM
Real success happens on your own terms.

We walked out of the hotel where the pageant had been held, just as the starlight was beginning to surface. Looking at the sparkling night sky above me, I took my mom's hand, and I realized I believed her. We'd find something for me, and it was okay that I didn't know what that thing was—*yet*. It is so easy to feel lost and alone when you're not sure what comes next in life. The not knowing can feel like there is a vast hole inside of you that you want to quickly fill up with everything and anything. I know that feeling—it's uncomfortable at best. But remember you can handle that discomfort. You can live with the not knowing for longer than you think. The night of that pageant I stood there looking at how the sky stretched for ages in all directions. It was so much bigger than little me and my giant trophy! The sky was like a heavenly reminder that there is a never-ending supply of choices and opportunities for us. You never have to settle for something that doesn't fit. There is always another option. Succeeding at any endeavor takes hard work, of course, but make sure you keep the faith, too—that there is room for you among that vast display of stars. Don't forget that you have the power to shine as brightly as any of them.

Chapter Two

Gold Lamé and Double Dutch

It's a classic storyline. A girl falls in love with acting and performs every chance she gets until her mother suggests they move to Los Angeles (along with her twin sister and little brother) to try to *make it BIG in show business.* Cue the excitement, heartbreak, drama, and harsh life lessons that can only be learned in that mission! I know this is not a new story, but my version does feature an important twist. My mother, practical as ever, gave us exactly one month to book something. We had to show that we had the passion to tackle Hollywood by landing a gig within those thirty days. No exceptions. If one of us didn't book a gig, we were packing up the car and hitting the road back to Texas. I played the role of confident fresh-faced wannabe actress perfectly, too. I was certain that any casting director looking at me would immediately grasp my warmth and wit and see how I would make the masses smile and laugh if they cast me. I was also convinced that after performing all over central Texas that I could tackle anything . . . Hollywood included.

Tia and I had been singing and dancing nonstop since the day my mother returned from running errands and handed over what was essentially a tween girl's dream come true in a shopping bag—leotards for both of us. From that day forward, our typical after-school routine of snack-procrastinate-homework-dawdle-chores was completed in a flash. I couldn't wait to practice our moves in the garage.

We practiced until the sun went down and Mom called us in to wash up for dinner using her "I'm not going to tell you twice" voice.

As the weeks passed, and we got better at those steps, we started to weave them together into a full-fledged routine. We danced along to the recording of "Rockin' Robin" by the Jackson 5 for hours—our mom coaching us. "Tamera, smile bigger. Tia, show more personality! C'mon, girls, you've got to stay in sync! I booked you a performance!" she said out of the blue one day. Tia and I stopped dancing midstep and looked at each other. While identical twins are not telepathic, the look we gave each other communicated, "Wait, she did what?" But the response we gave Mom was "Yes, ma'am!" Mom restarted the song. "That's right," she said. "You'll be performing two weeks from today at a county fair, so you've got to be ready."

There's nothing quite like the Texas summer heat that makes wearing any kind of costume utterly unbearable. Our cute little outfits from the mall, a white ruffled top and skirt set with purple polka dots looked so fresh when I put it on. But while I was standing still in a snap position waiting for the music to start, I felt my costume droop under the weight of my own sweat. It was dripping into every possible crack and crevice. *Gross.* Mom handed the emcee the cassette with our music. When the music started it only took a couple of notes for us to realize the wrong song was playing. Before Tia and I completely panicked, Mom had motioned to the DJ with a slashing motion across her neck—and then she mouthed, "Play the other side!" The DJ managed to get what Mom was saying. He flipped the cassette, and we started to dance again. We didn't dare show how embarrassed we were.

When folks heard Michael Jackson singing "Tweedle-lee-dee-dee," they looked up from their plates of potato salad and ribs to see a pair of identical sweat-soaked twins dancing for the sake of their lives. When we finished our routine the audience smiled and clapped loudly, Styrofoam plates balanced awkwardly in their laps. Our performance was so well received that we were each given a deep-fried Twinkie.

After that party, word spread around town that a pair of dancing twins would perform at gatherings (and they'd accept a Twinkie as payment). We wore out those sweet outfits performing at county fairs and community barbecues whenever we had the chance. Then we booked the mother of all local venues . . . the mall.

In the early '90s, the Killeen Mall wasn't just a shopping center. It was the After School Hot Spot. Kids from all over the popularity spectrum gathered under the bright neon lights of the food court to eat hot pretzels and judge each other for having bad skin or the wrong clothes. Our usual routine was not going to fly for this audience of angsty tweens and teens, and we knew it was critical that we up our sassy a couple of notches. We ditched Rockin' Robin and practiced our hip hop moves until we were in *Perfect Synchronicity*.

We put together a new look: Our pastel tutus were really taking things up a notch.

I felt a twinge of excitement every time I put it on, as if tulle had the power to transform me into a full-fledged star. A twin vision in tutus, we decided to call ourselves

"TnT Dynamite." You know, because we were explosive . . . get it?

Our mall performance was slated for a Saturday after-noon. This wasn't just prime time for family shopping. It was also when teenagers had the entire day free to roam around the mall, claws out and prepared to attack anything that wasn't cool. It was into this lion's den that we were going to bust out with moves like the Running Man and the Wop, decked out in our new pastel getups. We were either going to be eaten alive or queens of the pack after this performance.

Tia and I stood around nervously, sneaking peeks at the swarms of teens laughing and joking around with each other. I remember thinking, if they don't like us, we might have to pray to get the flu so we don't have to show our faces in school on Monday, When the music started and I heard that whispery voice saying, "Ahhh, push it," I took a deep breath, got a nose full of Cinnabon, and let the fear roll off my shoulders. We burst onto the stage singing, *Tia and Tamera here, and we're in effect.* As we worked through the choreography, our hips swinging, our tutus flounc-ing, people started gathering around the stage to watch, including some mall rats who had wandered over from the food court with their extra-large Orange Julius drinks.

My smile grew bigger as some of the spectators started to move to the beat along with us. As Tia and I struck a final pose, the people who had paused their Saturday shopping to watch us launched into hearty applause. We smiled and waved back, it was over. I was out of breath from dancing and flooded with relief that our performance was a hit and I could show myself at school the following Monday.

My mom was fully on board with her kids aiming high and harboring big dreams, and she did everything she could to support us. Mall gig number one multiplied into other mall gigs. We kept performing at county fairs where the applause was muffled by happy screams from the carnival rides. Tia and I auditioned for *Star Search*, and never even made it onto the show. I cried my eyes out after that rejection. Ever resourceful, Mom even managed to land us an agent in Dallas who booked us in small local commercials. So when we arrived in Los Angeles on a hot July afternoon, the clock on those thirty precious days already ticking, the sum total of our performance experiences had been nothing but positive. Our small Texas town had embraced us with a string of invites to perform and with gracious applause (and Twinkies).

This is the part of the story where the girl who moved to Hollywood to "make it big" gets hit with a dose of reality, so let's go ahead and get the analogy about little fishes and big ponds out of the way. We *knew* we were going to be little fish in a much bigger pond—we *wanted* to swim in the bigger pond! But after being hit with rejection after rejection we realized we were actually krill ... or maybe zooplankton. In the vast ocean that is the entertainment business, we were invisible. Compared to all the other exotic fish that were swimming around, our experience performing at malls and fairs now felt like a sad joke.

"Tia, I see you did a television commercial for the local fire department? Well, that's cute, but have you been in any Equity productions? Was the kind of response we were getting. As the rejections continued to pile up, the agent who had signed us said, "There just really aren't many parts for little Black girls, but you should keep trying."

After yet another day of auditions, we'd retreat back to the apartment where we were staying for the month. We'd eat dinner together, clean up, and practice the scenes we'd be performing for casting agents the next day. I ran my lines over and over, trying different approaches as if reading the lines "happier" or "funnier"—just being *a little extra* was the secret ticket to landing a job. I believed that if I was something *more* I could quiet the voice in my head that kept reminding me that I wasn't just a small fish, I was also a little Black girl, and *there just weren't many parts for me.*

Our time in Los Angeles was nearly up. We were

already down to our last few days. Hearing "no" on a daily basis hurt, but my desire to make the most of every minute I had in this crazy ocean was stronger than any rejection. I spent one morning in a room with Mom and Tia waiting to be called for what was probably going to be our last audition. The audition was for a Chrysler commercial, and we were expected to know how to double Dutch (we had no idea what jump roping had to do with cars). Neither of us knew how to double Dutch, but there was an elementary school right across the street from where we were staying. I walked up to the fence, a few girls were playing on the other side. I flat out asked, "Hi, can you double Dutch?" The girl looked at me like I had asked her if she had the ability to speak, but after a moment she smiled. "Yeah, I can." She said this with such pride that I got the feeling that this girl was some sort of jump rope maven.

"I'm Tamera. And this is my sister, Tia. We want to learn."

The jump rope maven looked me up and down, "Okay, Tamera, I'll teach you." We practiced every evening before dinner—learning to expertly get started by jumping between the two ropes. Once we got in there, the maven taught us how to hop from one foot to the other, jumping over each rope. We practiced until we were breathless, but we were confident that we could impress some car executives with our new skill.

When it was our turn at the audition, I smiled brightly and introduced myself: "Hi! I'm Tamera." I was asked to recite a line, and then it was my sister's turn. Tia did the same, then it was time to double dutch. We jumped like crazy, and just like that it was over. I walked out of the office wondering if my attempt at an acting career was over too. The phone call that I always wanted but never came finally came later that day as we were packing up our room, getting ready to head back home. It was Mom who answered the phone. "Tamera! Tia! Stop packing! The agent just called! You booked that Chrysler commercial! We can stay." *Cue twin girls jumping up and down and screaming!* Honestly, it was a miracle no one called the police. Tia and I can make quite a racket.

TAMERAISM
It's okay to fail as long as you fail up.

And this classic tale has a happy ending! Bring on the tiny chocolate hazelnut tortes! But like any true Hollywood story there will be many ups and downs to come. There wasn't a constant string of wins, but it didn't matter.

We were failing in the right place. Failure hurts, right? I'm not the first person to say, "Failure is part of the process, so here, have a cookie and cheer up." But I will say that you've gotta take a look at where you're failing! If you're in the big pond, then you need to give yourself kudos for getting in there at all. Failure might have nipped at you like a red garra fish,* but you've waded into that deep water and that's a huge start! Give yourself props for *failing up.* What you're doing takes guts! True, you could dominate in that smaller pond, but where's the satisfaction in that? Who cares if you need to swim up to the surface from time to time? Take a big breath of air, regroup, and get back in there because it's in the big lake that the big fish operate, and the big opportunities are floating around. And even though it might get scary, in your heart you know . . . *this is where I belong.*

---

*These are the fish, also known as *Garra rufa*, that like to eat dead human skin. Yes, they're the fish that are sometimes used for pedicures.

Chapter Three

Traffic and Homework

Every adventure has a first step, and sometimes the first steps are so small that we can barely recognize that a new journey has begun. Just seconds after we had set foot in our new rental apartment in Anaheim, California, Mom looked at me and said, "Tamera, go get the broom." The Mowry family moving ritual was always the same. We were transitioning into a new home with new possibilities, and that meant cleaning the space from top to bottom and *making it our own.* Our family was no stranger to big moves. I was born in Gelnhausen, Germany, a Christmas card of a village with an honest-to-God castle. Both of my parents were stationed there. When I was three my parents were transferred to Hawaii. My early childhood memories are marked by warm sand, gentle waves, and the perfection of Hawaii's rose-gold sunsets. Central Texas was next, and the shift from tropical paradise to long, dusty landscapes was *an adjustment*. But the move to the small two-bedroom in California was by far the biggest change. It wasn't just a new home; it was an entirely new life!

The first major shift. We had officially moved to California, but we were living separately from our father. Dad was still stationed in Texas, and Mom had left her job so she could make the move with us. Every morning after breakfast our sandwiches were packed in the ziplocks we had washed the night before. Reusing ziplocs and washing out disposable plastic cups was a small but constant reminder that the simple comforts that came along with being part of a two-income family had been cut in half and stretched to capacity. The Mowry kids were experiencing pockets of success here and there—we had all landed commercials and a few small parts, but nothing major. Money was tight and Hollywood was fickle, and that was a terrifying combination. Having no idea what was next was like riding a roller coaster with your eyes closed. Will there be a huge drop or a scary curve? Will I suddenly find myself upside down, hanging on for dear life? *What if I throw up?* Let me just go ahead and sum up what all those years of chasing success were like . . .

A Day in the Life of a Wannabe Tween Actress:

- Wake up and get dressed in short pants that you've outgrown. (There's no money for new, longer pants that fit!) You'll be made fun of for this.
- Eat generic cereal for breakfast and be grateful you have something to eat.
- Pack lunch, consisting of a sandwich with white bread and discount deli meat.
- Practice lines while sitting in traffic on way to school.
- Ignore eighth grade girl who asks, "Where's the flood?" when looking at your pants.
- School. School. School.
- After school: more traffic, running lines, and now, car sickness.
- Audition: this results in feeling either (1) you nailed it! or (2) you screwed it up.
- Homework in car, car sick again.
- Get call from agent about (1) job you booked or (2) job that rejected you.
- Decide to quit. This isn't for you.
- Chores, chores, dinner.
- Shower, and decide you will *never* ever quit no matter what!
- Pray that you land the next job.
- Sleep.

Repeat process for several years until *(1) you make it big or (2) you throw your hands and decide to be a regular kid. Regular kids do things like go to parties and get pizza with cute boys after school.*

The big chase finally stopped for us when my brother Tahj was cast on the sitcom *Full House*. While my brother played Teddy, the bff of Michelle, who was played by *both* Olsen twins, his real-life identical twin sisters were pulling an Olsen twins maneuver and splitting the role of Teddy's TV sister Denise. Got that? The episode we appeared in was called "The Devil Made Me Do It," and as far as I know no identical twins were mixed up during the shooting of that show. This is really something, considering that Tia and I had been temporarily put in charge of babysitting Mary Kate and Ashley on the set for half of a day. At first, I struggled to tell them apart (identical twins are not magically wired to be able to recognize the minute differences in other identical twins) but once I knew, *I knew*.

Now, to very quickly wrap up the multiyear saga about how I got my big break: Tahj, who was the Mowry kid who was cast the most, also did a show called *Out All Night* starring Patti LaBelle. (No! Seriously, I wasn't jealous at all. Success for one Mowry = success for us all, okay?). One of the producers on that show, a brilliant woman named Irene Dreayer, approached my mom one day on the set and asked, "Am I right that you have identical twin daughters? How come you didn't mention that before? I'd like to meet them." A meeting was set, but initially we didn't get our hopes up. We had been to enough so-called important meetings that we were jaded (well, slightly) by the time we were eleven. But when we sat down with Irene, all of my doubts popped like bubbles. She was elegant and smart, but kind and easy to talk to. She didn't treat us like kids; she treated us like smart humans who knew a thing or two. "What are your ideas?" she asked. "What do you two think would make a great show?"

No one in the industry had ever asked us what we thought before. In a rare moment of twin synchronicity we immediately blurted out, "*Sweet Valley High* meets *The Parent Trap!*"

She laughed and said, "Now that sounds like a show people would watch." People say kids are perceptive, and I swear I could feel something different in the air that day. Wanting to be an actress suddenly didn't feel like this outrageously impossible dream. It felt within reach because this woman seemed like she was on our side, that our ideas had value *because* we were kids.

This time we weren't trying to fit a producer's preconceived notion of what a character was like. Irene saw our spark; she saw something unique in us and wanted to tailor a show to fit that. *She was creating two roles for two Black girls.* She listened, and things were set in motion. Writers were brought in to discuss the idea, producers got involved, scripts were created, and eventually, after lots of meetings and some very painful nos at some major networks—ABC said yes.

Being cast on *Sister, Sister,* playing Tamera Campbell, was a gift that changed my life, and entering this exciting but challenging phase with my sister made it even better. Having her by my side made all the newness more manageable. The show became a big hit, and I suddenly became a familiar face in the homes of millions of Americans. I had to keep up with the routine of being on TV and balancing high school and work, and later college courses and work. We earned more money than we had in our lives, and Mom was thrilled that we'd changed the course of our futures. That's why I was surprised when at one of our first table reads, Mom leaned over to me and said, "You know, this is not going to last forever. What is happening right now is so special, but there is more to you and more to your life than this. It's who you are inside—your character that matters most."

Her words hit like a Category 4 hurricane, swooping in to wipe out the parade I'd been waiting years to see. All I heard was the negativity. But Mom was in the military, and she was known to tell us and everyone else how she saw things—straight with no chaser. She was simply planting the notion that someday this would end, and I'd have to go back to civilian life. She had zero intention of letting us become spoiled, out-of-touch, Hollywood actresses with no sense of reality. At that table read we were stars, but in life we were still her girls. Every night we still had the same basic schedule, but now it looked like this:

A DAY IN THE LIFE OF A WORKING TEEN ACTRESS
- Wake up and get dressed. Just put on something clean! Wardrobe will have something set out for you to wear at the studio.
- Eat breakfast, and try to get a little protein in there for endurance!
- Practice lines while sitting in traffic on way to the studio.
- Arrive at studio, and get changed in dressing room.
- Meet with producers and writers.
- Take gum out of mouth and stick on the wall before walking onto set to shoot.
- Break: do homework with tutor on set.
- Lunch from craft services.
- Run through lines with cast.
- Shoot more scenes.

- School. School. School. With the tutor. Get cookies from craft services.
- After school, more traffic, running lines, and again, car sickness. *Some things never change.*
- Chores, chores, dinner.
- Shower.
- Pray the show is a hit!
- Fall asleep the second the head hits that pillow.

Repeat process for several years *(hopefully) until the show is—I don't even want to say the word—c-a-n-c-e-l-e-d.*

We were the stars of *Sister, Sister,* a show that lasted seven seasons on syndicated television, but every day we were expected to keep the kitchen at home spotless, and our rooms clean enough to pass Mom's inspection every Friday. And Mom's inspections were no joke. Failing a Mom inspection and having to start over was the worst: it was so exhausting. But when you passed? The triumph felt huge, on par with summiting Mount Everest.

cele

Then when I was twenty-one years old, *Sister, Sister* was over . . . Just like that. I am not looking for piles of sympathy here, so there's no need to pull out your miniature violin. I had the unique experience of achieving success at a young age. I had managed to take some college classes while I was still on the show and would soon graduate with a degree in psychology from Pepperdine University. My entire life was ahead of me, yet it felt like it was already behind me. My love for acting didn't just die along with *Sister, Sister.* I now saw myself as a seasoned, experienced actress with a lot to offer, and I assumed the success from my youth would translate into a new success in my adulthood. But the phone never rang.

Long spells of nothing would be followed by an occasional audition, the end result being the same: "No, thank you." I auditioned for a drama I thought I was perfect for, and one of the producers looked me right in the eye and said, "Tamera, I really think you should stick to comedy." The roller-coaster ride that was my acting career seemed way too short, and now I was sweating it out in a never-ending line, with no idea if I would ever get a chance to get back on and ride again. The words "I'm not good enough" ran through my head on repeat. I couldn't think of any other explanation as to why I wasn't getting jobs. Eventually I had to face reality. Hollywood was breaking up with me!

Maybe I should start a support group for me and other kid actors? I imagined sitting in a circle discussing life with other talented kid actors from shows like The Brady Bunch, Facts of Life, and Full House.*

I'd have to find myself a new love. I had dipped my toes into other areas, but acting was my love interest. I had majored in psychology and thought about becoming a child psychologist. With our father stationed away from the family, Tia and I had ended up having a big hand in helping to raise our brothers. I was confident around little people and constantly amazed by their joy and creativity. I thought that could be an option in my post-acting life, but during a college internship I learned very quickly how difficult it is to see a child struggling with emotional pain.

I worked with a little boy I'll call "Kevin" He was ten years old and had suffered unspeakable tragedy. He was found alone in his father's home, and his father had been dead for three days. Kevin was put into foster care, and I remember him looking at me with his big brown eyes and saying, "No one will ever adopt me." He had already seen too much, and it was heartbreaking to meet a child who felt hopeless. Another boy I'll call "Nicholas" was an adorable nine-year-old with lots of spunk. He approached me

---

*I have had the pleasure of working with actors from some of these shows and they are fantastic.

one day and said, "Ms. Tamera, someone wrote 'Nicholas sucks' on the wall!"

"That's not very nice! Show me!" I said. Nicholas led me to the wall, and I immediately became suspicious about the fact that he was holding a pencil. "Nicholas, it's okay. But tell me, did you write that about yourself?"

He looked straight at me and said, "Yes."

Part of me wanted to wrap him in a big hug and tell him it was all going to be okay. A child that young dealing with depression and such low self-worth is tragic. But I need to be honest here. That day I knew if I pursued child psychology, I'd be carrying every child's pain as my own on a daily basis. Their pain would be with me as I drove home, cooked dinner, and ate. It would be with me when I went to sleep at night, and this was not something I was prepared to handle. I knew I didn't have the capacity to solve these kids' problems. I just didn't have the gift for this. I am in awe of the professionals who devote their lives to this important work, and I needed to be clear with myself that it wasn't something I was meant to do.

* * *

Tamera tests out new career choices! Take two! Child psychologist was out, but I became curious about teaching. I knew teaching would be a tough job, but this path felt like a better match for me. I could still make an impact on kids without having to navigate the tragic circumstances I encountered during the internship. I applied for a job as a kindergarten teacher at a private school, and I was feeling really good about the opportunity. Who says life stops after being on an award-winning sitcom? I could picture myself in my classroom. It would have tiny tables and chairs, and a cute corner to sit down in with a book. (I'd have perfectly organized bookshelves, obviously.) On the first day of school, I'd wear a cheerful dress, maybe yellow, and I'd write "Ms. Mowry" on the blackboard in colored chalk, maybe pink. I'd be just like Miss Honey from *Matilda*! Everyone loves Miss Honey. She's the quintessential grade schoolteacher! Life will be grand again!

When the phone rang one afternoon, I was excited to learn whether I had made it into the next step of the interview process. "Hi, Tamera! I'm so glad I caught you!" It was not the school principal. It was Mr. Hollywood agent, whom I hadn't heard from in a while. Now here he was, his voice dripping with enthusiasm. "Tamera, a really juicy role just came up, and you are perfect for it." Mr. Hollywood Agent went on to describe this new opportunity that had come out of nowhere. The role was indeed a good one—a doctor on a medical drama that took place at a women's medical clinic in Philadelphia. The character was a medical prodigy, inspired to become a doctor after her brother died in her arms after being shot. That's some rich character background for me to work with! *I'd play a doctor*, and I smiled at the thought. A doctor is a character with substance. I'd be a young boss lady this time, not a twin teen who fell into all sorts of antics. This would be a chance to test out my dramatic chops! I'd get to exercise an entirely different side of myself. Something inside of me was screaming, "This feels right!" But being a kindergarten teacher would also be so gratifying! But a doctor! *I'd love to play a doctor.*

I couldn't wait to tell my mom that her little girl might be swapping out the plaid pajamas from *Sister, Sister* for a white doctor's coat. But just as I was about to press the call button, I became terrified. I realized how badly I wanted this. I wanted it so badly I could taste it, smell it, see it, hear it, and feel it *everywhere*. Instead of calling my mom I sat down and had a conversation with myself. "Tamera, this is it. This is the role you've been dreaming about, and now it's here. There is *no* reason you can't get this role. You're ready, you have the talent, and you're good enough. Do not let any negative thoughts even enter your brain. Forget the previous rejections! They don't matter." When I was done giving myself a pep talk, I shifted my focus to *killing it* at the audition. They had seen my tape, but I needed to seal the deal in person. I had to tap into my inner Doogie Howser, my inner Susan Lewis and Meredith Grey—I'd conjure up the energy of every TV doctor who has graced the TV screen. I could practically picture myself in that white lab coat shouting things like, "We need blood, *stat!* or "Just stay with me! I'm not letting you die on this table!"

I woke up the morning of the audition feeling full of that energy. I swear for a second that if someone on the street shouted, "There's an emergency! We need a doctor!" I'd be able to run to their aid and save a life. Thankfully, that did not happen. No one was subjected to fake medical care in my pursuit to become a TV doctor.

I was practically bouncing up and down with excitement. As I was brewing coffee, I said out loud, to no one, "Let's do this!" Then I said it again as I got dressed— then one more time in the car. I repeated it while sitting in traffic, like a mantra. I said it once more while I was parking, while I was waiting for the elevator, while riding up on the elevator, and while waiting to be called into the audition. I. Was. Ready. When I heard "Tamera, it's your turn!" I practically burst into the room—it was *action time*. I stood poised and confident in front of the producers and said, "Let's do this." Apparently, the same mantra that had helped psyche me up for the audition came off with such assurance that not only did I get the part of Dr. Kayla Thornton, but that line became the first line my character ever spoke on the show. *Let's do this.*

TAMERAISM

There is no express train to success.

When Mom told me that "this won't last forever," what she really meant was that *Sister, Sister* was ultimately just one job in what would be a very long career. There would be more beginnings and more successes, and that also meant I could expect some drama and heartache in between. As nice as it would be, there is no high-speed, express train to success. You're going to make some stops, and not all of them are going to be scenic. Sometimes to get to your destination you will have to transfer. You might have to get off at a stop that's dark and scary while you wait for what's next. And there's no perfect timetable for success! It's hard to predict exactly when that next train will come. It could come really soon, or you might have to settle in for the long wait. But here's what I do know. Eventually another train will come. Success could be waiting for you at the very next stop, or you might have to transfer again. Who knows? The important thing is that you get back on the train. Climb aboard, take a seat, and enjoy the scenery because as long as you're moving forward, you're headed for something good. And I believe with all my heart that there is something spectacular waiting for you at the last stop. I don't know what it is, but I assure you the long, crazy ride will have been well worth it.

CHAPTER FOUR

Chewing Gum and Screaming People

Whenever Tia and I visited New York City when we were
starring in *Sister, Sister*, we always stayed at the Regal Royale
Hotel that was on 57th Street. (It's long gone.) Even as a
teen I loved the nonstop energy of New York City. There's
something about Manhattan that makes you feel that any
second something big and exciting is about to happen. We
had visited the city a few times, and our cousin Jerome was
with us on this trip. We were sitting in our hotel room,
high above the city where we could watch the never-ending
supply of cars and taxis snaking down the avenue. Just sitting in the hotel room with that big city right outside made
me feel itchy, like we were missing out on something. Suddenly I got a great idea. "Guys," I proposed, Let's go out,

just the three of us!" Tia and Jerome just looked at me as if I had said, "Let's walk down to Tiffany & Co. and rob the diamond vault." I was the girl who followed orders and didn't disobey. I added, "I know we aren't supposed to leave the hotel room without security, but what's the big deal? I just want to do something normal. Let's just walk to the corner store. I want some gum."

Walking a couple of blocks to buy a pack of gum sounded innocent enough, but I wanted to do it without Boo, who was our security guard. I wanted an all-out normal experience, and I didn't think there was anything normal about being accompanied by security. We got in the elevator and rode down to the lobby, nervous with excitement. *We're going walkin' around Manhattan—yay!*

I half expected my mother to materialize out of the air into the elevator and say, "Exactly where do you think you're going?" I breathed a sigh of relief when we made it to the lobby undetected. We were officially Mom-free and Boo-free.

When we pushed through the revolving door, the hustle and bustle of the city become the soundtrack to my first solo New York City adventure. We started walking, and I don't think I've ever felt so free. Everywhere I looked I saw stylish people rushing off to what I imagined were power lunches or important meetings. I wondered about all of them. The energy of the city was and is contagious, and could I picture a grown-up version of myself hailing taxis and scrambling to get *somewhere important*. We'd walked about a block when Jerome stopped us.

"Tia, Tamera, do you hear that?" We all stopped on the sidewalk. The crowds of people just kept moving past us. I thought I did hear something, but I wasn't not sure what it is.

Jerome started to look worried, and asked, "Seriously, what is that?" It sounded like Ssshhhhhhhhhhhhhhh... and the noise started to get closer and louder. Then Jerome saw something: "Look! Over there! They're headed this way."

There was a huge pack of teenagers running toward us. They were all shouting, "SISTER, SISTER, SISTER, SIS-TER," and it blended together into "Ssshhhhhhhhhhhhhh." Somehow someone recognized us, and apparently the word spread quickly.

They were running fast, and it occurred to me that this might be the reason we weren't supposed to leave the hotel without Boo. I stood there frozen, and the swarm of kids started to close in on us, and all could think was, *I am going to get in so much trouble.* Then, thankfully, Jerome was suddenly transformed into Kevin Costner from *The Bodyguard*.

"Run, this way!" He grabbed us each by the hand and started running down the street with us. As the sound of the pack grew louder, he said, "We just need to make it to the Duane Reade over there!"

Jerome opened the door, and we ran inside, Jerome yelling, "Move, move!" Jerome, who apparently could have had a future with the Secret Service, screamed at us to run to the back of the store. He jumped over the pharmacy counter like a seasoned spy, and we followed him, scurrying underneath the counter. We were crouched down near all of the cholesterol medication when the pharmacist spotted us. "You kids can't be back here! You've got to get out now!" I can't speak for Tia or Jerome, but I was terrified. I wasn't scared of the fans (even though it was a huge group) but of what my mother would do when she got a call from the NYPD: "Ma'am, I'm sorry to tell you this, but your daughters were arrested for trying to steal a vat of antibiotics at a midtown pharmacy. They will be held without bail until further notice."

I could not imagine how much trouble we were going to be in. The pharmacist's face was turning red with anger, and I was wondering if I'd have to spend the night in jail, or worse if my mom would kill me, when Jerome said, "C'mon, guys, it's okay." The pack was gone, and Jerome, who had apparently morphed into Ferris Bueller, and had no intention of going down for this nonsense, had managed to effortlessly sweet-talk the pharmacist into letting us go.

We made a beeline for our hotel and headed straight to our room. I was still shaking. Mom found out, because Boo was watching us the entire time and he called her. We thought we were being sneaky, but he had seen us leave the hotel. I got a talking to, but to be clear it wasn't because I was just being mischievous. It was because I had made a stupid choice, and I knew it. This was when I started to understand that there's a big difference between stepping out of your comfort zone and breaking away from your true character. And I had done the later. I was certainly old enough to handle walking a few blocks without a chaperone, but I should have known better than to purposefully ditch a man we were paying to keep us safe so I could feel like less of a goody two shoes.

Stepping out of my comfort zone meant singing on TV, trying new foods, and being open to playing a new role. Stepping away from my true character included the big things like disobeying or disrespecting my mother, and not being truthful. Walking down the street to buy gum wasn't going to go down as a moral failing for me, but I got a hint of how bad it can feel when my behavior didn't line up with what I felt was right in my heart. It felt shameful to disappoint my mother, and I never wanted to do it again.

TAMERAISM
Never break character.

It was a blessing to get an early glimpse of what breaking character felt like for me, because Hollywood, with all the glitzy parties, accolades, praise, big egos, and users, makes it easy for a young actress to forget who she is. I wanted to stay in the game of acting, but not if it meant of losing sight of who I was at my core.

A few years later I was put to the test. I was in conversations about a role in a film with a huge director who is known for his edgy and provocative films. Playing a role in one of his movies would have shown the world once and for all that there was much more to Tamera Mowry than sweet little Tamera Campbell. When I was told the role required a topless scene, I was done. That wasn't for me. Out of the question. I don't know what direction my career would have taken had I gone through with it, but the trade-off wasn't worth it. I chose to remain true to my character because doing so had kept me grounded, whole, balanced, and *happy* in an environment that eats up actresses like chew toys. I still like who I am, and this is what matters to me most.

I am fortunate to have survived working as a child

actress unscathed, because I am well aware that things haven't ended well for many young actors. Staying true to my character has been a guiding force for me, making it easier for me to make the right choices about my life and my career. If a role doesn't match my values, I step away and I never question the decision. And this Tameraism applies far beyond the playing fields of Hollywood. Staying true to your character in every area of your life and career matters and will make you a happier person. It doesn't complicate things, and you don't need to waver in your choices—let your character light the right path for you, and just follow it. It's a great way to stay focused on leading a self-fulfilling life. If something tries to pull you off that path, have faith in who you are and trust yourself! Whatever it is you're feeling is going to pass, so hang in there. Keep moving toward your light and never look back because liking who you see in the mirror is the greatest kindness you can give yourself.

THE PRESENT

*Now for our savory course, a plate of
ribs with all the fixings, including a
ridiculous fantasy date, dashed hopes,
and a summer romance served with a
side of self-love, all accompanied by a
glass of crisp, sparkling rosé from the
Why Is Dating So Difficult? region of
Northern California.*

CHAPTER FIVE

Cold Rosé and Romantic Comedies

I think we're ready to move on from careers and success to the topic of love, and that means one thing . . . wine. I think that chats about love and relationships pair best with a glass of crisp, cold rosé, wouldn't you agree? So let me get some glasses—and know that we'll need a generous pour for this one. People ask me about love and relationships a lot, and there was a time when I wanted to discuss this topic about as much as I wanted to have someone pluck out my eyelashes. This is because I got into the dating game so late, and I had no idea what I was doing. The lessons most people learned about romance in high school I didn't learn until much later since I spent most of my youth on a TV set. But now that I've been married for a few years and have had time to fully recover from the drama of it all, I'm up for the talk. We all have our own collection of dating stories, and it's likely they cover a range of genres. Rom-coms à la Nancy Meyers or Nora Ephron, scenes à la *Brown Sugar, Love and Basketball* . . . dramas worthy of Adrian Lyne (if you're thinking, *Wait, who?* two words: *Fatal Attraction*). If I were to make a movie about my dating life, it would be described like this:

It's Never Too Late for Love
Starring Tamera Mowry-Housley
Rated PG-13
Running time: 8 years
Will she get a boyfriend, or is she headed straight to spinsterville?
A young woman who grew up sheltered from the outside world embarks on a quest to find a relationship, only to discover that she is unaware of the bizarre rituals and rules required of dating as she learns to navigate the Fake Ass Date.

By the time I had the time to even consider dating I was woefully unprepared. I had no idea what to expect. The only real love I had experienced came from my parents, my grandmother, and of course Tia and my brothers. While that love is everything, it is also not at all the same. As I was growing up, I did imagine what dating would be like, and I would eventually learn that it had almost no basis in reality.

My teenage dream date was always the same. I'd be wearing white jeans, a flowy summer top, and cute sandals. My hair would be loose and natural, and I'd be wearing just enough makeup to show I made an effort. As I double-checked my teeth for runaway lip gloss and added a spritz of perfume, the doorbell would ring and my stomach would drop. *He's here.* I'd walk downstairs to find The Cutest Boy chatting with my mother. "It's so nice to finally meet you, Mrs. Mowry!" he'd be saying. He'd get ten extra points for impeccable manners! He'd promise to drive carefully and then walk me outside to his shiny bright-red convertible (a present for his sixteenth birthday—just like in the movies). He'd open the door, making a dramatic sweeping gesture, and declare, "Your chariot awaits you, pretty lady!" I'd smile up at him, my eyes twinkling, as he gently closed the door. He'd drive me to a carnival that is straight out of a teenage rom-com: bright lights, the sounds of young laughter, and the smells of everything fried.

We'd walk through the midway, our arms draped around each other's waists, and he'd look into my eyes and say, "Tamera, I am going to win you the biggest teddy bear at this carnival." I'd watch him throwing baseballs at a target, my eyes all agog as I saw his muscles flex with each toss of the ball. After winning a purple teddy bear the size of Texas, we'd walk over to the Ferris wheel, our teenage hearts practically beating out of our chests. We'd go around a few times, and then, because this was an imaginary date and therefore perfect—we would suddenly be stuck at the very top, hovering in the sky high above the carnival. That's when it would happen: he would lean in and kiss me. Cue brilliant firework display! (Stop with the eye roll—it was my fantasy and I was going for maximum romance). We would kiss under the glow of the fireworks and carnival lights until the Ferris wheel started moving again.

After our ride he would buy us bright pink cotton candy, which we would playfully stuff in each other's mouths—giggling at the silliness of it all. Then he would look at his watch and say, "Tamera, we've got to go. I promised your mother I'd get you home on time." We would drive home, the stars visible and the summer wind whipping my hair around as he went at *exactly* the speed limit. When we'd pull up to my house, he would do everything just right: he'd say he had a great time, he'd like to see me again, would it be okay if he called? Yes, yes, and yes. I'm walked to the front door and given a gentle goodnight kiss. I would get into bed, basking in the glow of *the best date ever* (and the moonlight would *of course* be streaming through the window). I'd fall asleep smiling, dreaming of those sweet cotton-candy kisses.

Sadly, my teenage fantasy wasn't the only date that never happened.

I'd learn after I went back to school at Pepperdine that the path to love is a very long and rocky one. As a child actress who spent her formative years working full time and cramming in her homework in between shoots, it was clear I hadn't even made it anywhere near the path. It was more like I was standing on the edge of a cliff looking down at all the romance and dating milestones I had missed, all of them crumbled up together in a big, messy pile including:

1. Crying at my locker between classes at school because a boy I liked didn't know I existed, while my ultra-stylish friend wearing fabulous shoes and a hat à la Alicia Silverstone in *Clueless* comforted me with the promise of shopping and a makeover.
2. Boy-girl group outings to horror movies that included flirtation in the form of playfully tossing popcorn at each other or grabbing someone's hand because a scene was just too scary!
3. Waiting by the phone—when would it ring? Would it ever ring?? "No one get on the phone because I

55

am expecting a call any minute now!" (I never had a chance to say that.)

4. Prom, aka the mother of all high school events. No one asked me to go, and I didn't have the courage to ask anyone to be my date. Alas, there are no prom pictures of Tamera Darvette Mowry wearing a colorful confection of a dress, staring happily into the camera next to a boy in a tuxedo wearing a matching cummerbund/bow tie combo after a very awkward attempt to affix a corsage to a strapless gown. *C'est la vie.*

By the time I started dating, my path to love was not only long, but paved with all kinds of ridiculousness: wearing sexy high heels even if they hurt my feet, stuffing myself into Spanx to look smoother and slimmer, buying nine different lipsticks in a quest to find that perfect shade of red (finally found it, ladies, Ruby Woo for the win!); the search for the quintessential little black dress that would look "effortless" when I wore it, even though the reality was it took ages to find; facials and waxing (the eyebrows as well as where the sun don't shine, even though I had no intentions of letting anyone go there); making sure my one annoying chin hair was plucked out; extending just about anything that can be extended—nails, eyelashes, hair; and, finally, ordering a salad even though what I really wanted was the ribs!

Perhaps the worst offender, ignoring an issue in a relationship that was the size of an elephant . . . because maybe things will change, or maybe it doesn't really matter! This leads us to what I want to share with you most of all, the crazy things we've all done to ourselves in the name of dating. Cue intro music. Enter the era of my dating life when I went on one Fake Ass Date after the other. If I were to make a movie about that period of my life, it would be described like this:

Fifty Fake Dates

Starring Tamera Mowry-Housley

Rated R (drinking, excessive hair straightening, and unreasonably high heels)

Running time: 2 years and 6 months.

What great lengths will a bright, intelligent woman go to in order to create a picture of perfection on a date, even if it means that she will end up loathing herself and her date?

In Fifty Fake Dates, *Tamera Mowry, the self-proclaimed queen of Fake Ass Dates, masters the art of hiding all her quirks, imperfections, and other normal human traits and replacing them with superficial qualities, unrealistic expectations, and uncomfortable shapewear. She looks pretty, but will the men know she's real?*

I am by no means a dating expert, but I suspect most of us have been on a Fake Ass Date or two. You know what I mean—those dates where you are so intent on putting your best foot forward that the person you present is a mere fraction of your true self? You want examples, eh?

1. Your getting-ready ritual includes watching hours of makeup tutorials on YouTube so you can totally change the look of your already perfect face.
2. You go to great lengths to ensure your hair is stick straight. You use straightening shampoo that costs more than a meal out, then you give yourself a blow dry that hurts because it wears out your arms quicker than an upper-body workout, and finally there's a once-over with a flat iron that is hotter than the surface of the sun. And success! Not even a hint of those beautiful natural curls can be seen!
3. Your Spanx are so tight that you're wondering if you can slip into the bathroom of the restaurant/bar/theatre and take them off and stuff them in your purse so you can breathe.
4. You're trying to remember if you have a pair of flip-flops in your car because the ultrasexy high heels you're wearing have already given you wicked blisters.

5. You're freaking out that your false eyelashes are going to fall off and land right in your Caesar salad. Now that's a garnish no one needs.

If you can relate to any of this, make no mistake, you were on a Fake Ass Date.

Alternatively, if you continue dating the guy who says he "doesn't want to have kids" even though you are positive that you want to have kids, please wake up and smell the Fake Ass Date.

No matter how much you might love the guy, you're not getting anywhere by not being true to you. The FAD is such an easy trap to fall into. I should know: there was a time when I'd crawl out of one trap just to fall right into another. Unlike most women who start learning the basics about dating in their teen years, I came at romance from a totally different place. I had thrown myself headfirst into my career when I was a girl, and when I came up for air I was somehow a grown woman who had *zero* experience with men, dating, and relationships. When I finally had time to try dating, I received quite an education in the form of dashed fantasies, unreasonable expectations, and wasted lip gloss.

FAD #1: My Classic Summer Romance

"Leonardo" was extra tall and shaggy haired, and he had the most adorable smile. We met on a Pepperdine travel abroad program to Florence. He initially got my attention by actually pulling my hair. His nickname for me was Palm Tree. The Hebrew meaning of "Tamera" is "date palm," and he thought it was perfection that my name meant "the sweet fruit that comes from a palm tree, the tree that can bend to withstand any storm." I interpreted this as he thought I was sweet enough to eat but also formidably strong. *How can a girl not respond to that?* Our young love bloomed over glasses of Brunello di Montalcino and shared plates of *pappardelle al ragù*, the local specialties. Walking through the streets of Florence, I thought I had died and gone to summer-abroad-college-romance heaven. I laughed so hard with Leonardo, and if he smiled I just melted into a puddle. Here's the interesting plot twist, though. Of the fifty students participating in this program from a Christian university, I fell for the one guy on the trip who was *not* into being a practicing Christian. Leonardo was technically Christian, but he was exploring New Age concepts. I figured that was Good Enough.

I soon realized that Good Enough wasn't right for me. I loved that Leonardo was so open-minded about religion, spirituality, and the big questions about life—but I'm a Jesus girl all the way. After long talks, I realized that Good Enough wasn't a path for me. Leonardo also knew our religious differences were a problem we weren't going to solve. I respect everyone's religious choices, but I needed a boyfriend who saw eye to eye with me on that. But I was so smitten I couldn't easily pull myself out of the relationship. Talking about leaving and really leaving were two different things. I even loved how he'd try to get my attention by stepping on the back of my shoe when we were walking down the street with a group of people from school. You know you like someone when annoying behavior suddenly = so cute! Please move on to FAD #2 to learn how to dive deeper into a FAD even if you know it's not right for you.

FAD #2: MY DARING GETAWAY

I was so out-of-my-mind boy crazy for this guy Leonardo that I tossed caution right into the wind and I up and ran off with him. It was spring break, and we hopped in his car and drove the nine hours to his parents' house in Arizona. It was so thrilling to be with him. Sometimes I had to look around to confirm it was really just us! Alone—the two of us, for hours on end with no one around, listening to music, laughing, and talking and talking, and driving off together. Those long hours of desert road flew by in a flash, and we bonded.

This was an especially daring move for me for a few reasons: (1) his parents were on vacation and the house would be empty; (2) I was a Christian girl whose values dictated that under no circumstances whatsoever would I be sleeping with him, even though we were alone in a big house; and (3) he did not share those same Christian values. Once again, I had to face the truth, that we just weren't walking on the same side of the street.

I remained true to myself on that vacation, but I knew I was in trouble the second I got home. Standing in the driveway was my mother. It was like a sixth sense had told her exactly when we were going to pull up. Her hands were on her hips, her foot was tapping with impatience, and her facial expression was easy to read . . . *I'd kill you if you weren't my own flesh and blood.* Worse than yelling at me, my mom was completely silent. I was ashamed I had let her down by going away with someone who I knew didn't share my values, and I saw how running off with Leonardo was ultimately a childish way to prove a point. I might have been running off with a man I loved who wasn't right for me . . . but eventually *you have to come back and face reality.* The issue of his religion was still staring us both in the face when we got home. Go to FAD #3 to learn more about making poor excuses for relationships, but prepare yourself for the fact that this saga with Leonardo doesn't end until I burst into tears at the college dance.

FAD #3: My Missionary Dating Period

If dressing to the nines and getting home from each date with blisters on your feet weren't enough, Missionary Dating is when you are involved with someone who has serious issues. First up on my list was a wonderful man, whom I'll call "Derek," who was an alcoholic. I adored Derek, but his addiction was something that required much more than the love of a good woman. He was a slick-talking-commitment-phobic bartender who was very easy on the eyes. When we'd hang out in clubs, which we did a lot in the beginning, this guy was drinking to excess . . . but, okay, so he likes to party. Nothin' wrong with that! Eventually I'd learn that, oh yes, there is something wrong with that!

We started doing datey things—hanging out at my house, cooking together, watching movies, and so on, and all of those at-home dating things also required loads of booze. Hmmmm. He also wasn't keen on taking me out in public. His ultracute bad boy vibe had completely blinded me to both of those big red flags. It eventually became clear that he wasn't just hanging with me. When he said, "I'm busy and can't get together," he actually meant, "I'm going to go out with another woman instead and post lots of pictures of her in a skimpy bikini."

If he didn't think I was smart enough to figure out that he was dating a bunch of women on the sly when he posted it all over social media? That definitely meant that he wasn't smart. *Next.*

If only I had known that the FADs—the dogs, the Good Enoughs, the disappointing Leonardos—were just one tiny corner of the big picture that became my love life! It would have been so much easier to blow off the ridiculousness if I accepted it as a steppingstone to the relationship I really wanted. We've all heard that famous quote, "Love conquers all." But c'mon—does it really? It's a fantasy to think love has the power to change someone's religion, beliefs, personality, vices, or addictions. Love can't conquer it all, but love *is* powerful. It can guide you to some wonderful places if you're true to yourself. Love is a place where you feel right, and no fake eyelashes or heavy-duty Spanx are required. Eventually I decided that I, Tamera Mowry, was officially done with Fake Ass Dates, as all of us should be. There are two questions people ask me all the time: (1) How did you meet Adam? and (2) How do you maintain a strong marriage? I'm writing this to the single and spoken for to let you know that it wasn't easy. True love isn't easy to come by, and dating is not always fun, but now I see that there's a little shortcut I could have taken. All of the dating would have been easier if I had focused on self-love first.

Enter the next and final phase of my love story . . . When I learned to love *myself*. The rules for this phase of the game are easy to follow, and they work whether you're looking to enjoy dating, find a partner, or strengthen the relationship you're already in. Here's some more good news: if you follow these rules you'll avoid ever having to use the phrase "it's complicated" when describing a relationship you're in ever again!

Stand in front of your mirror (hello, pretty you!) and raise your right hand. Now repeat after me.

"I [YOUR NAME HERE] swear to follow **Tamera's Seven Rules of Self-Love.**"

1. I know better than to think the length of my eyelashes or the size of my behind (or whatever body part or physical feature) is going to be The Thing that helps me land the right man.

2. I realize there is no shame in staying home with a good book and a pair of comfy pajamas. I don't need to do *everything* all the time! Please, FOMO is not something I can be bothered with.

3. I'll show my love by taking myself to the gym, feeding my body good food, and getting enough sleep.

4. I'll buy myself flowers and other treats because I deserve them.
5. I will dress like a gorgeous babe because *I want to.*
6. I'll make it a priority to spend time with my girl-friends laughing and enjoying life.
7. I will never lose sight of my value.

When I gave up the FADS and started focusing on me (who I already knew was awesome, but hey—we all need occasional reminders), I felt lighter. It was a relief to spend a night out with a friend at a bar or club and just focus on girlfriend fun. And I had lots of fun! Nothing casts a shadow over a girl's night out more than being stuck in *I-wonder-if-I'll-meet-someone-tonight mode.* Always whipping open your camera phone to check your hair, and your eyes wandering around the place. When I let myself step back and say, "It might not be my time to meet someone, but I know I will . . . eventually," I felt at peace. I had put myself in a place where I could enjoy the fantastic life I was currently living! I told myself that I'd still put my best foot forward if I met someone new, but I was going into each potential relationship knowing what I needed and wanted. For now, I was going to lean into the perks of being alone in my own life. I had independence, a great career, my own home, family, friends, my curiosity, and talent—all the things that I knew would make me a great partner to someone someday.

And then, finally, a light went off in my head. *Wouldn't being my authentic self be the best way to attract the man I wanted?* All that fakeness was just drawing the guys who couldn't deal with a real woman and a real relationship—and who needs a man who is scared off by everyday regular stuff? My straight-and-sleek going-out hair shouldn't be my big draw. I could finally see that the girl in the sneakers and the cute jeans with the natural hair had a lot to offer! And P.S.: she's not afraid to order the ribs.

TAMERAISM
The path to self-love is paved with ridiculousness.

Now that we're wrapping up this saga, I see I was too busy trying to find someone to love when I should have focused on loving myself. And that's just too important of a relationship to neglect! I believe that women are the stars of their own lives. The problem was that I was miscasting myself. I didn't stand a chance of hitting it big with *It's Never Too Late for Love* or *Fifty Fake Dates*—I wasn't in the right state of mind to carry those roles. It's so obvious now, but the role I needed to play first was in a movie called *The Woman She Loves Best*. It's a great story. It's about a young woman who is so comfortable and confident that she lives her life to the fullest, savoring every moment. She's a smart cookie, too—she knows she doesn't need a man to live her best life. She's already doing it! But when a man does show up? If he's good enough, maybe he'll get to be her costar. If he matches her vision for the picture that is her life? Well, then get set for a great sequel. And for those of you who are already hitched, you're not off the hook when it comes to self-love. The role of your leading man may have been cast, but you've got the rest of the movie to think about. If you want your film to be one of the Great Love Stories, that starts by loving yourself. You must understand deep in your soul that you are worthy and deserving of great love. You have everything it takes to make the movie you want, and, by the way, rosé pairs plenty well with popcorn. *So let me refill your glass!*

Chapter Six

Buttery Chardonnays, Luscious Reds, and a Scene from a First Date

Okay, brace yourself for another weird question! If you were a wine, what kind would you be? Maybe you're a Cava, always bubbly but also light and airy. A good Sauvignon Blanc can be fresh and racy—is that you? Or how about a Cabernet . . . spicy but smooth with depth. Me? I'm a red blend—a balance of spiciness and fruitiness. I'm sweet, but with a little bit of *bite*.

There are so many delicious wines out there—so many varieties of grapes! While not every wine is gonna be the right glass of wine for you, I'm confident that there is a wine to suit everyone's tastes. *Tamera, um, where exactly are you headed with this analogy?* Right! I'm getting there. The point I'm trying to get to is how I met my husband. As I've been saying, my career was in the right place, I had finally been dating correctly and was high on self-love, but I still hadn't had a real boyfriend. Also, let's face it: you can practice all the self-love you want, but it's not 100 percent guaranteed to save you from all the nonsense—the jerks, the guy who doesn't ask you a single question about yourself, the egomaniacs, the ghosters, or the cheaters. I might have viewed myself as a gorgeous crystal goblet ready to be filled with fine wine, so how was I ending up with nothing but overly sweet Kool-Aid? *Where exactly was all the good wine?* I had done the work on myself, but still nothing tasted quite right.

When I met the man who was to become my purpose partner, it didn't necessarily happen how I expected it to. Let me also say that as a woman who works in the wine industry, I have an appreciation for all varieties of wine. For the purposes of this story, however, I've opted to pair my wine and men as follows:

Tamera's Journey to Find a Purpose Partner

A Tasting Menu with Four Wine Pairings

Wine Pairing #1: Fake Ass Dates and Chateau de Bad Dates Chardonnay

This Chardonnay is as smooth and slick as butter and goes down easy but has afternotes of Axe cologne, mouthwash, and the air freshener that's been hanging on the rearview mirror of your car for the last five years.

Wine Pairing #2: Missionary Dating and Sauvignon Blanc, What Were You Thinking Cellars

This Sauvignon Blanc is extra fun with an explosion of fruit flavor, but finishes with notes of confusion, fear and misery.

Wine Pairing #3: The Purpose Partner and Cabernet, Oh, This Is What a Good Relationship Is Like! Vintners

This wine starts off with a gentle flavor, but slowly intensifies into something bold and interesting with an unexpected pop of sexiness. It finishes with notes of everlasting love (except for the one breakup that I will get to shortly).

Oh, Chardonnay can be a fun wine to drink (just like a FAD can be fun at first), but then I'd always end up with a big headache. The Sauvignon Blanc seemed so full of life upon first sip, but that wine quickly turned sour. I had nearly given up on wine. I felt I had tasted plenty, but was still ending up alone and sad. It occurred to me that perhaps I needed a palate cleanser, just a little time off from all the wine before I got back in the game. So when my favorite economics professor from Pepperdine offered me a blind date with a reporter he knew named Adam (let's think of him as a Cabernet), I almost didn't accept it. Now here's the story of my unremarkable (but ultimately life-changing) transition from Chardonnay drinker to Cabernet devotee:

1. *Adam, who is a correspondent for Fox News, goes to see his former economics professor, Professor X, while visiting the Pepperdine campus where we both went to college. Professor X also happens to be Tamera's favorite college professor.*
2. *Adam points to my picture (Professor X keeps photos of his favorite students on his wall, awwwww) and says, "I'd like to meet her."*
3. *Professor X confirms Adam has pointed to my photo and not the picture of Tia, my married twin who also took economics (it was a highly popular class). Professor X and Adam agree it's good he picked "the single sister."*

4. *Professor X emails me asking if he can give my number to the reporter. I respond no! I was temporarily done with dating! I needed a break to cleanse my palate. But I adore Professor X, and don't want to disappoint him. I tell Professor X he can pass along my email (I figure it's easier to let people down on email), and I just don't need another glass of wine right now.*

5. *Adam emails me, prefacing his message with "I never do this" (referring to emailing a strange woman out of the blue, I suppose), and I appreciate the sentiment. Adam asks if he can add me to the list of friends and family he sends his daily dispatch to, as he's now in Thailand covering the tragic tsunami. I'm surprised to discover that these emails are intelligent and insightful. I find myself looking forward to receiving emails from this very smart man who had put himself in harm's way to bring the world news of this important event (which is kind of hot). Somehow, we segue into a separate email conversation. We talk about life, what he's seeing in Thailand, my work, music, food, wine, family. A few emails later he says he's really enjoying our conversation and he'd like to take me out when he gets back. Hmmm, interesting—well, okay, I guess meeting him wouldn't hurt anything.*

Finally, we meet. This movie would be billed like this

The Uneventful First Date
Starring Tamera Mowry and Adam Housley
Rated G
Running time: 3 hours

And it would have a *very* uneventful first scene.

Scene 1 from *The Uneventful First Date*

"The Very Uneventful First Date"

Interior: PF Chang's, Early Evening
A young woman dressed casually in jeans and a T-shirt and a *very slightly* older, clean-shaven man in a button down shirt and rolled up khaki pants, sit across from each other in a large booth inside of a loud casual dining restaurant. They both pick up their water and take a drink at the exact same time. A waiter approaches.

WAITER
Can I interest you in some lettuce wraps or tempura calamari?

ADAM
Do you like red wine, Tamera? They have a good Cabernet on the wine list.

His face is completely hidden by an enormous menu.

TAMERA
Yes, I do.

A ding indicates Tamera is getting a text message. It is from her twin sister and reads, "What's he like?" Tamera quickly types back, "We are just going to be friends." Tamera smiles at Adam.

WAITER
Okay, so a bottle of Cabernet, and are you ready
to order?

TAMERA
I'll have the dynamite shrimp to start, and the
Mongolian beef, please."

ADAM
I'll have the pad Thai with shrimp.

Waiter nods and walks off to put in their order. The couple continue making small talk and enjoy a pleasant conversation while eating their meals.

And the reviews would look like this:

Rom-Com Monthly—"Totally accurate depiction of a normal first date." Rating: Four out of four hearts.

Dating Digest—"Drama-free and uneventful, just like a first date should be! Rating: Perfect movie to watch alone if you're not going on a date, or with a date while on a date.

Hopeful Single Press—"*The Uneventful First Date* shows us that a dinner date can indeed lead to a second date that is also so unremarkable that neither party will remember what the second date was."

If you are thinking, *That is the most boring date I've ever read about in my life! Your lame movie is not going to be trending on Netflix anytime soon, Tamera! Where's the chemistry? Where's the action? Can you at least have an ex show up and start a fight with Adam that results in fisticuffs? Or maybe there's a fire and the restaurant is engulfed in flames and Adam saves you by carrying you out? Or vice versa? Something, anything else!*

DING DING DING! You score fifty points for having the right response! This wasn't exactly a thrill fest, and that's the point. There was no drama, no big excitement, no massive butterflies. No red wine was spilled during the fictional recap of my first date with my husband. It was a *totally normal* evening, which wasn't at all what I was used to, because this time I was out with a sophisticated and respectful Cab man, and not another smooth-like-butter Chardonnay that just ends up doing me wrong. We talked. We exchanged pleasantries and information about our lives. We ate dinner. We listened to each other.

Here's where things get interesting. Something started to happen as the evening progressed. I forgot I was on a date. I was just enjoying having a conversation with an intelligent, interesting, and kind man. I found myself wanting a bit more of this Cabernet guy. I wasn't thinking about how much I wanted to make out. I was thinking, *I want to be in the presence of this person.* It was a hint to me that this could lead to more than friendship (contrary to what I was texting Tia). And here is the uneventful, unexciting, not terribly romantic but absolutely life-changing thing about dating that no one ever talks about . . . *sometimes the spark comes along a little bit later.* Sometimes you are drawn to the person for who they are first!

I can't even be sure of what we were talking about— church, food, movies, acting, or his job as a correspondent are likely topics. I'm telling you this Cab went with everything! It went down so effortlessly that when we finally realized the waiter was giving us the side-eye for overstaying and it was time to go, we moved the conversation to the car. You know what happened in that car? Not kissing, I do not do that on the first date. We talked more! We listened to music and a couple of hours flew right by.

When I got home that night I slipped into my favorite jammies. (I barely had to wash my face—I didn't even bother with makeup that night.) I climbed into bed and reflected on the evening. It was so pleasant, so stress-free! *But is it weird that I feel totally normal?* I thought to myself. *I'm not all freaked out about when I'm going to see him. I'm not preoccupied about whether or not he likes me.* That's when it occurred to me that everything was so nice, so pleasant, so very comfortable—and this was the *polar opposite* of everything I was used to. It was so normal that it felt weird. I pulled the covers up to my chin and fell into a peaceful sleep. I woke up the next morning and made myself a cup of coffee and thought, *Huh, that Cabernet sure went down well last night. Whoa, is it possible that I have found my flavor? Why haven't I been open to red wines before?*

TAMERAISM
Choose your people like you choose your wine.

If you want to find a purpose partner, you've got to develop your palate. You need to be open to new flavors no matter how crazy (leather, pepper) or boring (berries, apples) they sound at first. I spent years messing around with Chardonnays and Sauvignon Blancs, but had I paid more attention to the varieties of grapes *in my own life* I could have figured out I was destined to be a Cabernet drinker sooner. Some of my favorite flavors had been right in front of me the entire time. My twin, Tia, and my cousin Jerome have big, bright, juicy personalities like a Petite Syrah. I'd use the words "wise" and "bold" to describe my grandmother Cloretha, who was as regal and as special as an Old Vine Zinfandel.

It turns out I needed a purpose partner who was fun and full of personality, who was grounded by wisdom, but who also brought his own special quality to the mix. When I met Adam, he brought a brand-new layer of flavor into my already sweet life. He is fun and wise, but he's also complex, dependable, and fulfilling. My Adam is like an Estate Cabernet Sauvignon, and he was the secret ingredient I was waiting for all along. It would be quite a few years before we were ready for the final wine pairing, but I can tell you that when we finally got there it exceeded all my expectations.

Wine Pairing #4: Marriage and Adam and Tamera's Field Blend, Housley's Century Oak Winery

This wine is a mix of three beautiful grapes, the Petite Syrah, Old Vine Zinfandel, and Estate Cabernet Sauvignon. This ideal blend finishes with the flavors of an engagement in Venice, a wedding, a house in Napa Valley, a son and daughter, careers, dreams, traveling, holidays, traditions, rituals, meals, baking, barbeques, birthday parties, and a dog.

My path to finding my purpose partner was long and complicated. At times I was so frustrated by the bad dates and the disappointments I experienced along the way that I just wanted to scream at the top of my lungs, "WHERE ARE YOU? ARE YOU OUT THERE SOMEWHERE?" Now, as I enter my second decade of marriage, I see that relationships (much like a great wine) just can't be rushed. It takes time to create the right level of tart and sweet. It takes work to balance the laughter and light. Finding the flavors is just the beginning. It takes constant effort and adjustment to keep everything balanced. A relationship needs to be properly tended to because if you're not careful, things can turn sour. But we're purposeful about our love and our relationship. We cultivate the goodness and toss out the occasional sour grape because we are in it for the long haul. Our marriage will get better and bolder with age, and like a truly great wine we intend to savor every drop.

BONUS FEATURE:

DELETED SCENE FROM *THE UNEVENTFUL FIRST DATE*

"The Horseback Ride Gone Crazy"

It was a warm autumn day when I saddled up my horse Admiral for my horseback riding lesson. I walked him from the stable to the bridle path that led through some gently sloping hills. I gave him a snuggle to the face and climbed onto the saddle. We started walking along the path, the sun projecting a soft glow over everything. A few minutes later the instructor told me to urge him into a light gallop, the gorgeous landscape of California unfolding before us. The route we were following was beautiful. I was enjoying the view and the fresh air, and I felt content for the first time in a long time. The breakup with Adam was taking its toll in a big way. Adam and I decided to take time off to rethink the relationship, and the break up was taking a toll in a big way.

The oneness between myself and this gorgeous creature with whom I am sharing the afternoon is perfection. Suddenly, this horse decided he's had enough. This six-hundred-plus-creature has decided he will be heading back to the barn right now and I am coming along with him.

Before I fully comprehend what's happening, he's running full speed ahead off the path. I try to remain calm—but he clearly has the power now. He hauls himself over fallen trees and gains speed as we fly down another hill.

My joyful morning ride is replaced with terror, and I have no choice but to trust him and trust myself to hold on tight enough. He runs into a dense thicket of trees. I lean into him, ducking down below the tree branches, and I hold on tight. If I'm going to get back to the stable in once piece, I have no choice but to just duck and trust. I accept that he's in charge now, and I give myself completely over. As we continue running through the forest my fear starts to evaporate. We keep running. I'm still holding on, I'm still alive, and I start to feel incredibly free. After a few more minutes the ride becomes exhilarating. Soon enough we're back into our original rhythm as horse and rider, and we're walking slowly. I'm relieved, and once again I'm able to take in the beautiful day as we get closer to the stable (and the joyful feeling of being alive!). When Admiral gets us back to the stable I climb off. I'm still shaken by the experience, but for Admiral the moment is over as he happily munches on an apple. The horse isn't thinking about whether or not he had a near-death experience. He's not picturing the headlines that could have been: "Tamera Mowry, Teen Star of *Sister, Sister*, Tragically Runs off Edge of Cliff with Horse During Riding Lesson." Admiral trusted his instincts, followed them, and we both survived.

If you've ever ridden a horse you probably know that the experience can be both exhilarating and terrifying. Horses are the most intuitive and gentle creatures, but to have a successful ride there needs to be trust and control. Hold the reins too loose, and that horse will go wherever it wants—maybe alongside the road to eat an appealing patch of grass or for a wild run. You can pull up on the reins to get him back under your command, but if you're not holding him tight—if you do not *have control,* he's the one taking you for a ride. But when you're in charge, that horse knows it, and that connection can be a beautiful thing. Feeling that freedom and being at one with another creature . . . there's nothing like it. But sometimes you're not in sync with the horse, and that's where things can get scary.

During that time the heartbreak was hurting in a way I had never experienced. Some days the particularly tender pain of it took over everything—other days I managed to rein it in. Weeks had gone by, but the ache persisted. Was this feeling ever going to leave me? Is this how women become "cat people"? I looked at Admiral, happily drinking the water in his trough. I almost envied his ability to live in the moment. *Is it possible there was a lesson to be learned from this horse who nearly killed me?* Of course it's possible! In romcoms people learn from animals all the time! *So what was the lesson, Tamera?*

It would take a highly skilled director to create a scene where a young woman in the throes of heartbreak is set straight by a manic horse. How do you do that without dialogue? I suppose one approach is the voiceover. Picture me on the big screen as Admiral drags me through the forest. (Who am I kidding? It would be a stunt person.)

BONUS FEATURE:

NARRATION FROM *THE UNEVENTFUL FIRST DATE*

"The Horseback Ride Gone Crazy: Epilogue"

Voiceover by Queen Latifah

Sometimes to have a truly joyful experience you have to both let go and hang on. Some of the scariest moments of our lives are frightening because we don't know what's next. This is true whether you're flying through the countryside on a huge animal, trying to build a career, dating, or you've just agreed to commit yourself—mind, body, and soul to one person. Admitting to yourself that you want a relationship. You need to get comfortable with telling God, "please, I want a partner and a family—I want it all even though it's scary!" You can't know what comes next. You pray for health, children, success, and joy. But like that insane horse, you can't always control what life throws at you. One minute you're riding along and all is well, and then in a flash a that horse throws everything into a big mess and there is no way to know, and it was time to accept that there were no sure answers. There was no guarantee I'd meet someone, but that's not a reason to end the ride.

But I had survived that ride. So maybe it would be okay to just "duck and trust" when it came to finding a purpose partner. I started to think both that I was holding on too tight and that I needed to relinquish control. I had to learn to enjoy *the entire* ride (even the truly terrifying parts). I needed to have faith that I'd be fine. I walked up to Admiral and gave him a rub on the nose and one last carrot before I said goodbye. I'd be back soon.

In this scene, the sun glowing orange as it was starting to set, there would be a shot of me walking away. The narrator Queen Latifah would say: "Enjoy the ride and know that you'll be fine. And when things feel like they're just too much, duck and trust, because sometimes it's the best way to get through the wild, unpredictable terrain that is life."

Chapter Seven

Snow Pants and Hot Chocolate

I hate skiing. I hate everything about it. I don't like cold weather (although as a fan of Christmas I do appreciate snow). I don't like all of the heavy layers of clothes required to stay warm. I don't like how hard it is to pee when you are wearing snow pants. I can't stand how difficult it is to walk in snow boots. And when your nose starts to run (which it does constantly in the cold) it's a pain to pull off your glove to dig around for a tissue. And can we talk about the sun shining off all that snow? *It's blinding!* You can't see a thing! If I'm going to be romping around on a mountain, I'd like to be able to see *exactly* where the edge is, thank you very much. I feel terrified on the ski lift, and I feel terrified getting off the ski lift. I don't like how I feel lumbering and awkward on skis...like a polar version of Frankenstein. Oh! And here's a question. Why are there trees smack dab in the middle of the mountain? So you can break your fall by slamming your body directly into a tree? I'm sorry, I really don't like to be negative, but I'm afraid there's more. It's hard not to be intimidated by the better skiers, especially the ones who are about six years old. I can actually feel their resentment oozing out of the snow they kick in my direction as they fly past me. The whoosh-whoosh of their skis screams, "Get off this mountain, slow lady!" As they make their way down the mountain like Olympians. And to wrap up this little tirade—I just don't enjoy the feel of cold wind whipping at my face as I try to navigate myself down a mountain without breaking every bone in my body...It just doesn't feel like freedom to me. More like a near-death experience. To clarify: skiing is not my favorite activity.

All I can tell you is that I did not know I was signing up for this by marrying Adam Housley. Adam is a secular man. I don't mean he's secular in a religious sense. It's like he's secular *about life*. The man does not follow one code of living—he's up for anything. Whether it is skiing black diamonds or watching the sunset at the beach, he wants to do it all. Let me give you an example. Adam and I are opening a charming little coffee shop in Napa. Think soft lighting, cozy chairs and sofas, a place to enjoy a cappuccino and pain au chocolate while you kick back with a good novel. Knowing Adam, every cappuccino will be an exercise in perfection with a top-notch espresso-steam-foam-milk situation. And that beautiful cup of coffee will not only be handed to you with love . . . It will be topped off with masterful cappuccino art that accurately depicts your toddler.

Now let's look at the other end of the spectrum. Adam is an intrepid reporter. Toss Adam into a war zone and he'll manage just fine. (Venezuela might be the one exception. The president banned Adam from ever setting foot in the country again, unless he wants to be hunted down and arrested.) Adam can transition from Ernest Hemingway on assignment to a full-fledged metrosexual at the drop of a hat . . . whether that hat is your basic baseball cap or a handsome fedora.

I love the dichotomy of Adam, and I'm into the flavor and zest it adds to my life and to my family. I try to meet him in this being-up-for-anything-place whenever I can. Then he took me skiing.

I do not like to feel out of control or vulnerable, and it seems to me that venturing to the top of a snowy mountain with long, slippery sticks attached to your feet with the intention of sliding to the bottom is the definition of vulnerability. But every winter I agree (reluctantly) to take a ski trip with my family. As a mother it terrifies me to watch Aden and Ariah learn to navigate the slopes, but I force myself not to stop them because I know that learning to tackle a mountain is also learning to manage the feeling of being out of control. And in my heart of hearts, as I watch all my loves skiing, I know that the four of us wouldn't be together if I hadn't had the courage to get over myself and let my guard down many years ago.

A few years into our relationship Adam and I broke up. Why we broke up isn't something I like to discuss, so can we please leave it at this? There was a time when we faced some challenges that felt insurmountable . . . and let's just say that it resulted in a long pause in our relationship. Please pass the tissues! Just thinking about that time makes me cry. Do you see my eyes welling up? So let's keep going with this story. After Adam and I called it quits I entered what I now refer to as the "party-fast-pray" period of my life. My heart and my head were a messed-up cocktail of hurt and confusion, garnished with some heavy, ugly anger. I was heartbroken and adrift, scared of never finding love again, and angry—at Adam, at myself, and at the world. Why didn't our relationship work? Was there something wrong with me? I tried to be strong, I tried to stay positive, but the hurt took over everything.

Fine. *If I'm single*, I thought, *I am going to be a bad girl.* I'd get dressed up in my version of skimpy. I even felt like

I failed at this—I'd do sequins but nothing tight or short. When I felt like being really racy, I'd put on an off-the-shoulder top. I was clubbing with my dear friends Andrea and Cheri, and sometimes my brother Tahj. Just thinking about the hardcore cocktails I drank back then makes me feel sick. Can you believe I actually drank a concoction called the Orgasm? One night after a few "orgasms" it was time to go home, but somehow the valet had managed to lose my keys. I was *messed up*, but not messed up enough to remember that Adam still had a set of my keys. I was definitely going to use this as an excuse to call him. "Guys, I need to call Adam!" I told my friends. Thankfully, I barely remember that night, Adam, always the gentlemen picked me up and got me home safely. In the end it was just another sad night of partying to try to push my pain away.

I'd wake up after clubbing hungover, dehydrated, puffy-eyed, and sad. I felt even lower than if I had just stayed home and acted out any of the post-breakup clichés; spending the entire day in my pajamas, watching rom-coms snuggled up with a pint of ice cream, or throwing back a few glasses of red and popcorn while examining Adam's social media feeds for clues. Was he going out? Was he seeing someone? Did he look miserable and sad because we were not together? Feeling awful all around after a big night out, I'd tell myself it was time to pull it together . . . Then I'd have a revelation. The answer to all of this is heart ache was *self-care*. I'd toss the wine and Ben & Jerry's in the trash. *My body was a temple!* I'd stock up on organic kale, green apples, celery, lemons, and big knobs of spicy gingerroot. Green juice for the win! I'd get my butt back into the Pilates studio, coaxing my soul back to a happy place with every single round of the hundreds.

While self-care is crucial, it didn't mask the hurt. I wasn't allowing myself to heal properly, and until I got brave enough to look inward, I wasn't going to get better. I pray regularly, but desperate to feel like I was back on solid ground, I'd pray more. I have had broken hearts before. The first time I lost a big love, Leonardo, I didn't think I'd survive the breakup, but I did. The pain I felt when I ran into him with another girl in his arms on the dance floor at a party on campus was extreme. I felt like I had been punched in the face . . . and in the gut. *How could he have moved on already? And so quickly?* Watching them, I felt my lip quivering, and the tears were threatening to pour out of my eyes in front of everyone. Just as I was preparing to march up to him and tell him what I thought of him, my cousin Jerome had his arm gently around me. "Let's get you home, Tamera."

Thankfully, Jerome was there to usher me out before I could make a total fool out of myself. He sat by my side all night as I sobbed, only stopping long enough to pro-claim dramatically, "I'll never feel that much love again!" He handed me another tissue and looked straight into my bloodshot eyes. "Tamera, I know you're hurting, and I'm sorry. But listen, you can't let this take over your life. He's not worth it. So I'll tell you what . . . I'm going to give you three days. You have three days to cry, eat junk food, and be as sad as you need to be. Throw things if you want! But then it all ends. You've got to get on with your life!" I snif-fled and nodded; few people knew me as well as Jerome. The sobfest continued in earnest—my mascara-stained tears permanently staining the shoulder of Jerome's shirt. But then it was Day Three. I got out of bed, took a shower, found the eyedrops, put on a cute outfit, and got on with my life. I certainly wasn't over it, far from it—but I was engaged in my life again. Jerome had put me on the path to becoming my old self.

When it came to my breakup with Adam, it had been sooooo much longer than three days, and the tactic that had slowly healed my heart back in college wasn't making a dent in my pain. Why was this so different? The scariest bit was that I had developed a habit of drinking an entire bottle of wine alone by myself. Memories of my time with Adam ran through my head with each sip. How he patiently and kindly taught me all about wine—the different grapes, how they're grown, the wonderful subtleties of different flavors. He introduced me to his loving family, and I felt right at home with his parents and brother and the beautiful life they had built in Napa. I didn't like baseball, and Adam even played professionally for a while after college, but now that seemed like something I could easily get over! He supported my big dreams and he never doubted that acting was the right path for me. He was one of my top supporters, urging me to stay focused on my dream even though it was so challenging at times. I knew he'd never let me give up, and I was willing to do whatever it took to support his vision for a well-lived life.

And how it hurt to remember what I missed most of all! Adam sitting beside me in church, his hand reaching for mine during the sermon. We weren't just going to church together, we were sharing our vision of a purposeful life—God-focused, dream-centered, with plenty of room for love, growth, laughter, wine, and someday (or so I thought), marriage and family. As I remembered what it felt like to be in church, surrounded by God, completely at peace with myself and my life because The Man of My Dreams was beside me, I started to cry. Again. This was a big hurt, and I couldn't see any way out of it but through it.

It's Sunday morning a few weeks later, and I'm on my way to the late service at the church Adam and I used to go to together in Los Angeles. Since we broke up, we've been attending church at different times. I walk inside, and the usher tells me, "I know where there's an empty seat. I'll show you." I follow the usher, who leads me to the single, empty seat in a church that feels big enough to host the Oscars. "Here you go," he says quietly, pointing to a vacant seat. I feel the breath leave my body. Sitting right next to that empty seat is Adam. My heart is pumping, I feel a tingle at the back of my neck, and I am positively flooded with emotions . . . fear, excitement, and most of all, hope. I want to say something, everything—what I've been doing, how I've been feeling. I want to ask him a bunch of questions: Is it true that he's still actually hanging out with my brother even though we broke up? Is he seeing anyone? But most important, I want to tell him how much I miss him, and that I love him and *I need him in my life*. While all of this is running through my head, I realize I'm still standing in the aisle—frozen. Adam looks at me and smiles. *Does this man have any idea how much I've been hurting?* I'm trying to conjure up the courage to speak, to say anything—but the connection from my brain to my mouth has somehow been disconnected. *Get it together! You've been crying your eyes out over this man! Staying out late, partying, drinking, and eating ice cream. You know how you feel! This is not the time to be coy. If you want this man back in your life, you're going to have to get vulnerable!*

I turn toward Adam, and I say, "Are you dating anyone?" I got the words out before I could become too afraid of his answer to speak. He looks up and says, "No. I'm not." I smile back at him, and I sit down. The air all around me feels different. I often feel peaceful in church, but this is a different kind of peace. I feel like I have another chance to build a life with a man I love—with an honest-to-God purpose partner. When I was with Adam it was like the sun was shining down on me, and for the first time in too long, the light looks golden again.

After church we decide to get brunch at our favorite spot. I'm buzzing with as much excitement as a little kid on Christmas morning. We fall back into our old routine, coffee, pancakes for Adam, and an egg scramble with veggies for me. We are both nervous, and Adam breaks the ice by saying, "What are the odds that that was the only available seat?"

We talk openly and honestly about our feelings, how much we missed each other. I am so happy, and I feel like I'm home. This brunch is as warm as fresh apple pie and just-baked cookies, and I never want it to end. Then we get to the big question . . . "Do you want to try this again?" Adam says, "If we're going to do this, I need to know you're all in. So, Tamera, is this what you want?" I smile. It is all that I want.

cele

I am on top of a mountain with my skis on, and while it's terrifying how high up we are, the view really is something. *If I die at least it will be in such a pretty place!* I try to squash the negative thoughts—they aren't helping. I remind myself I made it to the top, and that's a great start. I was tempted to stay in the lodge, drinking cocoa by the fire—but I didn't want to be the odd Housley out. If my children and husband have the courage to fly down a mountain, I can do it, too, so I sign up for skiing lessons. I had to put my big pants (snow pants, actually) on and face my fear. It's a fear I swear the instructor can smell, and he asks, "Do you trust me, Tamera?" I nod my head; my life is in his hands! "Tamera, the trick is to visualize where you want to go, and your skis will follow you there," I start to move forward, as slowly as I possibly can—but I can't seem to stop myself from looking toward the edge of the mountain. It's like I need assurance that I'm not going to fall off. "Tamera! Don't look that way, you're navigating yourself toward the wrong side. Have faith. Look forward and move forward." I realize that I need to shift my focus from what could happen (plunging off a cliff) to what is *actually* happening. I start again, visualizing the trail in front of me. I slowly start to descend. As

I continue to visualize where I want to go, I make steady progress. *I'm doing it!* I haven't lost control—I've let go of my fear. I'm moving, but I'm still the one in charge. I spend the next one and half hours navigating my way down the mountain. I don't crash into a tree, I don't get run over (nor do I plow down any other skiers), and I don't plunge off the side—I've made it to the bottom intact.

TAMERAISM
You need to look where you want to go.

At the bottom of the mountain, I eventually find my family, who had just finished a more advanced run. "Mommy! You did it!" The kids are thrilled, and Adam gives me a quick kiss and asks, "You want to go down again?" I look toward the lodge where there is a warm fire, warm drinks, and an extra plush sofa that I could easily sink into. The idea of taking off these crazy boots and kicking back in front of a fire is appealing, but where's the challenge in that? It's important to be safe and warm sometimes, but it's also important to *get off that sofa and get real about what you want.* Whether it's getting down a mountain so you can enjoy time with your family, or applying for that job, telling someone how you feel, dating again, following your dream! The most important things in life—love, success, family, dreams—aren't delivered to your front door in a package wrapped up with a tidy bow. You have to go get them. You've got to get vulnerable and open yourself up to the possibility! And yes, you could get a big fat *no thank you* or an *I'm sorry I just don't feel this is a good fit*. It could hurt, and I've been there! But I want you to trust me here. Because you could also get exactly what you want! The difference between marrying the man of your dreams or not . . . the difference between landing that big promotion instead of staying exactly where you are is *getting vulnerable*. You have the power to tackle any mountain. The magic is in you. You just need to visualize where you want to go and let yourself follow suit.

BONUS FEATURE:

DELETED SCENE FROM *THE UNEVENTFUL FIRST DATE*

"The Trip to Paris"

THURSDAY MORNING

Adam was calling all the way from Jerusalem, but he sounded like he was right there. I really wished that true because I really missed him. "Tamera, I have an idea. It's kind of crazy. What if we meet in Paris?"

Cue to me wanting to shout, "YES, YES, YES, YES," but I forced myself to stop and let it all run through my head first. *Can I just drop everything and run off to a foreign country to see a man? We haven't been together that long. But wait. What's "that long?" Girl, it's been long enough! Traveling with someone can be intense. We'll learn a lot about each other. Do I want him to know that much about me already? Duck and trust, girl! Remember that?*

"Yes, let's do it!" I shout.

Plans are made. Tickets are purchased, and we are able to arrange it so that both of our flights get into Paris at the same time. We will meet at the airport and run off together to a chic boutique hotel in the heart of the city. We'll walk around arm in arm, buying baguettes and crois-sants. We'll eat out in quaint bistros—with candles and bottles of wine. We'll look at artistic masterpieces and visit cathedrals. Our love will be so palpable to the citizens of Paris that that jazzy, charming French music will follow us around everywhere we go. The only thing that will be missing from this scenario are striped shirts and berets, a tiny dog, and a pack of cigarettes (neither of us smokes).

With Paris on my mind, I go shopping. It's fall, and I'm dreaming of rich cashmere sweaters and classic black pants. French women don't mess around, and I splurge on the chicest sweater—grey cashmere. Asymmetrical. I am going to look *hot*. As I wander around the department store, my eyes are drawn to the perfect item to top off my

Lady in Paris with Her Man look. Thigh-high boots, caramel colored. Rich and luxurious but also ooh la la—sexy. After giving my credit card quite a workout, I go home to pack.

FRIDAY, 10 A.M.

I am practically bouncing up and down in the car on the way to the airport. I spent, wow, two hours blowing out my hair into straight Parisian elegance. *C'est très jolie.* I put on my beautiful new sweater and zip my legs into sassy boots. ADAM, HERE I COME! There is only an eleven-hour flight between me and *mon coeur.*

SOMEWHERE OVER THE ATLANTIC OCEAN . . .

I watch a film, enjoy a glass of red wine, and eat some dark chocolate. I'm all happy inside thinking about my romantic and spontaneous vacation. I decide to take a beauty nap so I'll look my best when I see Adam at the airport. I picture us seeing each other from opposite ends of the terminal. We run into each other's arms. Adam will drop his luggage and pick me up in the air and twirl me around. *Alors* our reunion is *très charmant.* Sooooooo charming that we actually appear to be moving in slow motion to everyone else in the airport. Love is in the air.

I wake up from my nap. Hmmm. I'm kind of hot. Maybe wearing thigh-high leather boots on an international flight wasn't the best idea? Come to think of it, it's so hot on this plane that I'm sweating. I wish I had a T-shirt underneath this sweater. I need water. It's too hot.

Meanwhile, Over in Israel

Attention, please!

Attention! To any of you lovestruck individuals who are catching the flight to Paris to meet your girlfriend. We regret to inform you that your flight is delayed (for undisclosed reasons) for four hours (maybe more, who knows?). We sincerely hope that this does not have any impact on the romantic factor of your trip. We realize that smartphones have not been invented yet and you have no way to inform Tamera that you will be late. Good luck, and we hope she won't be mad.

Paris, Charles de Gaulle Airport

I get off the plan at who the hell knows what time. Months, years, decades could have gone by, the flight felt so long, especially in leather boots that cover my entire body.

I stagger out of the plane. I cannot wait to see Adam. I make my way through customs feeling more and more impatient. *Mon amour* awaits!

CUSTOMS OFFICER
Mademoiselle, what is the reason for your visit to France, *si'l vous plait?*

TAMERA

I'm here to relish in the fact that I've found everlasting love, and I'm planning to flaunt my romance all over your city of lights!

With a thunk, he stamps my passport—it feels like the nation of France is verifying our love. I make my way to baggage claim. I'm tapping my foot inside of the inferno that is my thigh-high boot while I wait for the baggage carousel to start moving. *Why. Is. This. Taking. So. Longgg...?* Finally, I see my suitcase. Picking it up requires all of my strength. I had to pack a lot of cute outfit options. I drag my suitcase (*Damn, this is heavy! Did someone stash a body in here when I wasn't looking?*) over toward the exit, where I am finally going to meet Adam. I'm a little out of breath by the time I get there.

There is no Adam.

A half an hour later there is still no Adam.

WHERE IS ADAM?

I drag my bag to the information desk. I learn that his flight is indeed late. I decide to meet him closer to his terminal, which requires riding a tram and dragging my bag what feels like several hundred miles. I'm sweating. Sweat is pouring down my face. I look around at all the poised, elegant women carrying small bags—all of them wearing amazing sunglasses. *Seriously, what is their secret? How is it possible that French women don't sweat? Perhaps they just perspire lightly? Also, how do they tie their scarves like that?*

I decide to freshen up in the ladies' room before Adam's plane gets in. What I see in the mirror is not Parisian chic. My makeup has run down my face, my elegant cashmere sweater is crumpled like a wet dog, and my hair—the hair I had perfected especially for this romantic journey is half straight and half curly. I have managed to simultaneously look like the "before" and "after" pictures of a makeover.

I fix myself up as much as possible and go out to greet Adam's plane. From the other end of the terminal, I see a fresh-faced, energetic, and adorable man running toward me. IT'S ADAM! IT'S ADAM! He easily scoops me up into an embrace...because the only luggage he has is a backpack. How is that even possible? Lesson to be learned on this trip? Men can travel internationally with two shirts and one pair of pants. The injustice!! But now our romantic vacay can begin in earnest!

CUT TO INTERIOR: Elegant room in a chic boutique hotel. There is a view of the Eiffel tour outside of the tall window.* A disheveled young Black woman is rummaging around in her suitcase frantically searching for something.

> TAMERA
> Voila! I found my flat iron! I cannot imagine going to dinner with this crazy hair.

Young woman is about to insert plug of flatiron into electrical socket. All that is holding her back from a perfect dinner is her crazy, out-of-control hair.

> ADAM
> Sweetie, I wouldn't do that if I was. . . .

There is a loud pop, and voilà. All of the lights go out. The couple are standing in semidarkness. The only light in the room is coming from the outside.

> TAMERA
> Um, I think I blew a fuse?

There is a knock at the door. Adam opens it to find a distressed hotel worker.

---

* Okay, I admit it. Our hotel did not have a view of *La Tour Eiffel*. But it obviously would in the movie version, so please just go with it.

DISTRESSED HOTEL WORKER
Bonsoir. Um, *Je suis désolé. Alors . . .* , all of the,
how do you say . . . Power? Is out in *l'hôtel.* We
do not know how long it will take to be restored.
J'excuse.

Distressed hotel worker smiles and shuts the door.

TAMERA
Oh, wow. So I suppose when you were saying not to
plug that in, this is why? Did he just say I blew out
the power for the entire hotel? For everyone?

ADAM
Yeah, he sure did. Can we get going before they
find it was the Americans who took out the elec-
tricity? We need to leave if we want to make our
reservation.

Shot of young woman in mirror staring at her half-curled/
half-straight hair. She stares at herself for a few seconds,
then starts rummaging through a cosmetics bag.

Then, from inside of bathroom, she calls out.

TAMERA
I'm ready to go! I hope you like my hair.

Interior of small, intimate restaurant in Paris. A couple
stares at each other over candles while drinking wine.
They smile at each other.

Camera zooms in to woman. She's wearing an elegant sweater and big earrings. She has a huge smile on her face. Her hair is in two pigtails, which creates the effect of her looking like a tween among the highly polished women of Paris.

Our trip didn't exactly go as expected, but it was also one of the most important journeys of my life. Traveling with a beaux is like the big reveal of the relationship. You can't hide much when you're in a foreign country where you don't speak the language, you're staying in a small room, and you're navigating unknown territory together. Traveling and seeing the world is a wondrous thing—being able to still love your boyfriend and have him still love you after taking out the power of an entire hotel? That's priceless. I wish there was more of a point to this outtake—I wish I had some wise words to impart after having a fancy dinner in Paris in pigtails (other than don't ride a plane in your thigh-high boots). If there is any point to this story it's this: real love is so far from perfect. Just as with traveling, there are always lots of surprises in love, and you have a choice to make. Do I accept this man fully and unconditionally even though he refuses to ask for directions when we've obviously been lost for two hours? Do I accept this woman even though it will take double the time to walk to dinner because she's just gotta wear high heels? That refusal to ask for directions might turn into an inability to put socks in the dirty laundry.

Humans, even the ones we love desperately, can be a little annoying. I said it! But the part that matters is this: when you finally get to that restaurant (albeit late) and you take a breath and sit down and accept a glass of wine from the waiter, are you sitting across from the person who makes your soul light up? If your soul lights up, forget the directions, the pigtails, and the shoes. Just clink glasses and get on with it . . . because there are so many more adventures for you to have, and you can plan on none of them being perfect. That's love.

Chapter Eight

Inner Hotness and Sex Goals

Before we get into all this, I need you to do me a little favor. For a minute, can you please imagine the following scenario: You are out in the world. You're just going about your life, maybe you're running errands, or you're on your way home from the gym. You think, *An iced coffee would be nice right about now.* You decide to pop in to a coffee shop. You buy your drink, and because you don't have to be anywhere in the next half hour you plop yourself down in a chair. Maybe you check your phone or take advantage of the free time to catch up on your book club reading. You're flying through chapter 3, but then a complete stranger sits down next to you and starts asking some ultra-*ultra*personal questions about your sex life. You'd probably feel weird, freaked out, and maybe even a little violated, right? I'd be willing to bet my favorite pair of big earrings that you'd think, *Um, and why exactly is this any of your business?* Am I right? Why would you talk about one the most sacred and personal aspects of your body and soul with a total stranger?

(To be clear: I'm not saying this exact scenario happened to me. I'm an actress—I'm using a dramatization to demonstrate a point, people!)

As a woman of faith who literally grew up in front of the camera, there has always been speculation about my sex life. Seriously, why ya'll want to know about my cooch? First of all, there's the wholesome thing. *Tamera is so wholesome. Therefore she must be a prude!* This is a common conclusion people draw about me. *Prude.* You know who called me a prude first? My brother. Thanks, Tahj Just the word itself is displeasing! It conjures up images of a wrinkled, cranky old witch who lives in the depths of some faraway forest with a troll. Just because there are details I keep between myself and my husband does not automatically put me in the prude category. For the record, I'm not a prude. Fun fact about me: I am a true Freak in the Sheets—go ahead and do what you want with that information.

The second thing people wonder about is when I actually started having sex. People—I'm talking strangers on the street!—have flat out have asked me, "Did you remain true to your Christian values before you got married?" Seriously? Let's briefly go back to that coffee shop scenario. What would you do if someone asked you to discuss the who/when/how/why of your very first sexual experience? I highly doubt you'd lean forward eagerly and say, "Well, it was great actually. It happened on a fluffy cloud with the world's most perfect person after we got married in a castle. The sky filled with rainbows afterward! Thanks for asking, and enjoy your day!" You wouldn't answer the question because it's highly inappropriate and no one's business but your own.

I have been asked to talk about these things, in interviews and on *The Real*—and it's not something I have ever felt comfortable doing. And let me just add that more people have watched *The Real* than you could fit into every Starbucks in Northern California. So, take that fictional conversation with the nosy stranger and multiply it by several million.

While my sexuality is a very important part of who I am, I don't think it's anyone's right to ask those questions just because they watched me on TV when they were a teen, or because I was on a talk show.

But we're not asking you, Tamera! This is your book, and you're the one who brought up the topic. We're just readers who are along for the ride.

Fair point.

I bring up the topic of sex because it is important to me, and there are a few things I'd like to say about it. I'm by no means an expert on this topic, but I do want to share that as a happily married woman I feel sex is a key part of maintaining a strong connection. I'm certainly not going to tell you what to do or how to do it—nor do you need to know the ins and outs (now there's an award-winning double entendre) of what goes on in my life/bedroom/closet. But as fellow human beings, as *fellow women*—I think we deserve healthy, loving relationships that also happen to involve great sex. So let's get into it.

1. Inner Hotness Is the Right Kind of Hot

We've all been physically attracted to someone *because they're attractive*, but a set of six-pack abs will only get you so far. Whether it's muscles, a thick head of hair, a strong jawline, or sparkling eyes that float our boat, that doesn't mean the object of your attraction really has what it takes to keep that spark flying. We've all had empty attractions, and they don't do us any good.

Yes, obviously, a person can be superhot as well as kind, brilliant, and caring! My point is that it's the inner goods that will keep a flame going. A set of deep sparkling eyes isn't going to be sexy forever if you don't actually like the human those eyes belong to. The inner person must be hot! I think my husband is hot inside and out, and that's what keeps us going. I didn't fall in love with his face (although it's adorable and handsome). It was his character that really got me going. Respect and kindness—yes, please! Patience and intelligence, oh yes. Bring. It. On. It's not the six-pack that provides support when you've had a rotten day; it's the human that comes along with it who has the power to make your day brighter. *And that's what's hot.* To all the married ladies: sometimes you might have to remind yourself what's hot about your husband. The next time he brings you a cup of coffee or rubs your feet after a long day at work, take a minute to think about how sexy that is!

I'll add that just because I'm married I didn't stop noticing hot men—you don't go blind after you tie the knot.

But hotness can instantly evaporate with a dumb comment or some dog behavior. Outer hotness will not remain hot if it's not attached to a kind and supportive man.

2. Know What Kind of Meal You Want

If you've ever opened a magazine, you've read the same old advice about how it's important to know what you like in bed and to be able to share your needs with your partner.

We need to move on from the conversation about who does what to whom and what gets put where. I'm talking about what kind of relationship and life you envision for yourself. Do you want a relationship in which sex is one of the main courses? If you view sex like a nutritious and fortifying meal that you need regularly to be your best self—then make that known to your partner. Have that conversation about how often you need that hot, regular meal and what that meal should consist of.

I also understand not everyone wants to eat all of the time. Some people are fine skipping out on dinner! Maybe for you sex is an occasional, super-sweet, ultraspecial dessert. Just have that discussion. Come to a mutually satisfactory agreement on how often you'd like to dine together and what you want mealtime to be like.

3. Sex Is Healing

Have you ever just felt stressed or had a really bad day and then you remember, *Oh, I think there's a big bar of rich dark chocolate in the pantry. That's exactly what I need right now!* Chocolate is a wonderful thing, and sure, it can lift your spirits—but only temporarily. I say to you all, "Put down the chocolate (or ice cream, red wine, jellybeans, potato chips, or whatever your go-to stress snack is) and get busy with your partner." Sometimes Adam will find me in my closet—it's a refuge for me. My closet is a clean and well-organized space where I can quietly collect my thoughts. (Several portions of this book were in fact written in my closet.) If I'm in there long enough he knows it means I had a difficult day. He'll walk in, rub my shoulders, and quietly whisper, "I know something that can make you feel better," and off we go. Or more accurately, off we go postbedtime. Such is the lay of the land when you have kids. (Sometimes morning sex is actually the best way to go.) See what happens when you start to think of sex as the answer to your woes. Reconnecting with your partner physically is the best and most fun way to remind yourself, *I'm not alone in what I'm feeling. I'm connected with this person who cares about me.*

And let's be real—human beings can be annoying. Adam is my best friend, my true other half, but that doesn't mean he doesn't occasionally get on my last nerve. This is another good reason to have sex. It can be a reminder that you love your partner *even though they are a grown person who can't remember to put their socks in the hamper.* I urge you to recast sex as a mechanism for healing. Chocolate cannot listen to your problems. Chocolate cannot remind you that "Hey, it's you and me against the world." Chocolate cannot discuss your dreams and insecurities with you.

4. HAVE SEX GOALS

My life philosophy has been to grow more, do more, take risks, and challenge myself! And my life and career have expanded to wonderful new places as a result. I've always been the kind of person who wants to know *what's next?* So I set goals and take the steps to accomplish them. I want to see the world, I want to produce more movies, I want to raise a family, I want our family wine business to thrive. I always take a moment to appreciate my accomplishments and the blessings I've had—but then I think about how things can go to the next level. My marriage is one of the most important things in my life, so I have high expectations for our physical relationship too. That's why I have a list of the places I'd like to have sex. It's an ongoing list that I add to regularly, and I find it keeps things *really* interesting. And no, I'm not going to share which items have been happily checked off, but I will share that "on an airplane" will never make the list—too small of a space and way too many germs. But you handle the friendly skies as you see fit. My list looks like this:

1. The shower
2. On top of the car in the rain (the rain is a key part of this fantasy)

3. Every room in the house

4. The backseat of a convertible

5. Every continent

6. On a private beach on a private island with the waves lapping at my feet

7. Under a fluffy duvet in a quaint bed and breakfast in the middle of the afternoon, ideally with picturesque fall foliage at its peak

8. Luxury hotels

9. The woods

10. The swimming pool

11. The rooftop of a skyscraper with a great view

12. On a picnic blanket in a field of lavender (it's my list, don't judge me)

13. My closet (surrounded by all the shoes, possibly while wearing shoes)

TAMERAISM

If you want to keep a relationship spicy,
update your list of sex goals.

Sex is beautifully intense, and it is one of God's greatest gifts to human beings. And as a woman who has treated sex carefully and has made it a priority in her life, I just want to say this to you: Embrace your sexuality. Learn what you want, explore everything you want to explore, and enjoy the person you are sharing your life with. Put the chocolate down, throw out the ice cream, make that list, get crazy, and have fun together. Ultimately, I just want you to remember that when it comes to making a satisfying meal there are unlimited ingredients. You can cook up something spicy or something sweet. You can prepare a long, slow meal with several courses, or, if you'd prefer, just a quick snack or an extra-indulgent dessert every now and then. Just make sure you're getting the meal you want, and ideally, you'll have a relationship in which no one goes hungry.

THE FUTURE

We'll finish off our time together with a

selection of house-made minidesserts,

such as fear-of-flying cheesecakes,

chocolate-walnut-flavored job anxiety,

and our famous mommy guilt topped

with a dollop of crème fraiche.

CHAPTER NINE

Pancakes and a Second Cup of Coffee

When you're in the throes of love, the sun never shines brighter, right? The world is so full of wonders that it practically glows. At this particular stage in my life, I was surrounded by the love I needed, but I was experiencing an entirely new heartbreak, and it happened every single Sunday.

During this Sunday heartbreak marathon, on weekend mornings I got to wake up in my own house, in my bed, next to my husband, with my children sleeping right down the hall. The sunshine that peeks through the windows is a delight, the smell of familiar bedsheets equals perfection, and the sound of four tiny feet headed in my direction is the Sweetest Thing. Fresh from a good sleep, the kids are already full of energy and demanding pancakes. When we get up, we'll have the kind of big family breakfast that's only possible on weekends. Adam flipping pancakes, sticky syrup dripping onto the table from sticky hands, and the freedom to linger over a second cup of coffee. Already hyper, the kids jump in our bed and scurry under the duvet for a cuddle. I breathe in, and it's like falling in love with the smell of these cute babies all over again.

When the Sunday scaries started a few years ago I'd still have these moments, but now every other Sunday was shadowed by a harsh and steady anxiety. I could be happily playing with the kids, and then suddenly—it takes over. When it happens, I have to wipe away a tear and pull my focus back to my kids who are just happy that Mommy is home. I need to keep it together, because the thing about Sundays is that they are *way* too short. Though I try to act like Sundays still have their own personality, they are really just an express ride to Monday morning.

Our late breakfast is followed by a long walk into town. The weather is perfect, and the streets of Napa are bustling with tourists visiting tasting rooms, sampling jewel-toned reds and golden Chardonnays. The sound of friends, couples and families laughing together makes me feel desperate to just stay put instead of taking my usual pilgrimage to LA. As I let myself indulge in a quick fantasy of not having to go to work quite yet, the fickle Napa Valley sunshine is taken over by fog. The sun that warmed my shoulders like a perfect sweater suddenly dips behind a mountain, and I shiver from the chill. The drop in temperature is an unpleasant reminder that the afternoon will soon become evening. It is already time to go home and pack, kiss my husband and kids goodbye again, and get my butt to the airport so I can be thrown back into the whirlwind that is my job on a daytime talk show.

To be clear, this isn't about an inner battle about working or not working, and I know it's a privilege to even contemplate having that battle. I love working, but I think we can all agree the push and pull of it can be painful. And as the years went by during my time as a cohost on the hit show *The Real*, it became clear the job was holding me back, and the environment was becoming toxic. I'll get into all that later, after we're fully caffeinated and ready to transition to a bold red.

When we walk in the door after our Sunday walk, everything happens in a flurry. I scribble out some notes to Adam—he handles everything when I'm gone. I grab the suitcase that never gets put away and start to pack while Adam finds my dry cleaning. Big earrings, shoes, Spanx, workout clothes, iPad, chargers, makeup . . . check!

I'm looking around for the new scented candle I bought

(because a touch of home in my dressing room never hurts!) when I feel an unwelcome wave of sickness. *Oh no. Tamera, you are not going to throw up from nerves again! You are a grown woman with responsibilities, and you need to get over yourself and go to work! Your family can manage the week without you. P.S. The plane has not crashed yet!*

I spot the vanilla-scented candle on the other side of my room, but by now I'm running to the bathroom with my hands over my mouth—I'm definitely going to be sick. As I brush my teeth and splash cold water on my face after yet another one of my Sunday episodes, I think about what my life was like before I was on *The Real*. I remember saying to myself, "A talk show? How hard could it be?" Those were the famous last words of a woman who had no idea what she was getting herself into. And I'll also add that I underestimated how terrified I would be flying on the tiny commuter plane back and forth between Napa and Los Angeles every week. Looking back, I'd say a fair share of the weekly throw-up sessions were due to fear of the impending flight. If you've watched *The Real*, and I hope you have because it's a terrific show, you might be thinking, *Seriously? Because you looked perfectly fine on TV. You never looked ill! And it seemed like y'all were getting along just great!* You're right. From the outside looking in, the show looked like a casual chat between a group of smart women—but the reality for me was quite different.

I'm a warrior. I've never needed things to be easy, but as a talk show host I felt like I was failing constantly. I always seemed to say the wrong thing—my foot was constantly in my mouth. It's like I'd find a piece of this crazy puzzle . . . stop saying this, don't smile too much, don't *not* smile, make your point! Then I'd be presented with a fresh new challenge. *Oh . . . so if I don't interrupt someone else when they are speaking, I don't get an opportunity to share my opinion and I am ultimately just sitting here silent like I have nothing to say!!!* At first, it felt impossible to break into the conversation. To get an opinion in among five intelligent and articulate women was hard enough, but for a girl who was taught not to interrupt when others are speaking it was nearly impossible. You want to be heard on a talk show? Then you practically need to shout. There were times I literally raised my hand.

You finally get to make a point? Prepare yourself for the fact that if the world doesn't agree with you, they're going to let you know. Every day felt like I was putting another opportunity out there for the world to judge me for speaking my own truth. My words would get twisted and turned until it was not at all what I said. No matter what we were talking about there never seemed to be a shortage of cruel comments thrown my way afterward. I looked polished, poised, and in control sitting at that table with my colleagues, but inside I was a mess. It was a lot like getting strapped into a roller coaster—you're up for a thrilling ride, and you actually like the butterflies in your stomach. This is going to be an exciting new adventure! But just as the announcer tells you to always keep your hands inside the car, you take off and you're shot out into space, *and that's it*. It's dark, you don't know where you are, you don't know when it's going to end, and you just want to scream You're flying loose and fast through space thinking, *This is not what I signed up for.*

As an actress I had experienced plenty of scrutiny, but having my personal beliefs criticized felt like a direct attack on my soul. I wasn't reading off of a script; it was who I was as a person, and some people would get lethal. It was hard to swallow every single attack, at least for me, and there was no thickening of my skin. I was who I was, and people were not happy to hear what I had to say. I'm glad that there are people in the world who can handle a machine gun aimed and loaded for their personal character, but not me!

I knew from experience exactly how much damage all of this negativity could do to my psyche. When I was a teenager, it was "just words" that resulted in my feeling badly about myself. When starring on *Sister, Sister,* Tia and I adored getting fan mail. That people liked the show enough to take the time to write letters to us was mind-blowing. We were full of gratitude and made a sisterly pact to read and respond to every letter. One day after a long week of shooting, we were sitting on my bed in our pajamas looking through the pillowcase that we always used to bring the fan mail home in, and it was stuffed full. We cued up our favorite music, set ourselves up with snacks, and gathered up our colorful pens so we could sign eight-by-ten glossies to send to fans. I emptied out the pillowcase, and dozens of envelopes of all shapes and sizes fluttered out. We waded through a pile of letters that were addressed to "Tia and Tamera," most of them kind, simply saying how much they liked the show or how special it was to see other Black kids on television. Then Tia handed over a plain white envelope addressed specifically to me. I grabbed a cherry Twizzler and opened the letter.

Dear Tamera,

 I've been watching your show every week, and I want you to know that I think you are UGLY and goofy.

I read the words over again. The second time I read them it just hurt more. I was ugly *and* goofy? What a horrible combination! I looked over at Tia, my *identical* twin who was *not ugly*. Was there something about my face just different enough to make me the ugly sister? When I read the word "goofy" I immediately branded myself as awkward and lumbering. Suddenly, in my mind, I was like a gap-toothed cartoon dog with a weird voice and gigantic feet. I was showing up in the living rooms of millions of other teenagers each week on television as the ugly and goofy twin. I was the girl who stayed home on Friday nights while the pretty sister went out! I tried to remember the last time I got invited to a party and couldn't. Was I not getting invited to parties because I was the silly and weird one? *Do people think I'm a freak?* Worst of all, I was convinced that prom was off the table, because no one wants to go to prom with the goofy girl. Everyone wants to go with the prom queen! The moment I read that letter the perception I had of myself as a kind, fun, and perfectly normal-looking girl was blown. I was ugly and goofy, and not once did it occur to me to doubt the truth of a total stranger's words.

Many years went by, and there were many successes I was proud of. I won an NAACP award and was nominated for a People's Choice Award. And after winning three orange blimps I'm in the Kids' Choice Hall of Fame. I have a golden blimp! Oddly enough, I have never had the experience of being drenched in buckets full of thick neon-green slime. How did I miss out on that classic Nickelodeon rite of passage?

I made movies both with and without my sister and graduated from college. But through it all, I was still Ugly and Goofy in my head. Ugly and Goofy were like two evil twin personalities fighting in my head for domination. Let's see, am I Ugly today? No, actually today I'm just Goofy. Whether I woke up feeling Ugly or Goofy, or some terrible combo of the two, their constant presence made it easier for me to doubt myself. Anything that didn't go right with my life—if I didn't get a part I wanted or a second date didn't follow a first, I was certain that Ugly and Goofy were responsible. There was never a way to get them off my tail either, and they were absolutely relentless when I was working on *The Real*.

During a long, chatty brunch with my good friend Andrea, I finally admitted to her how badly I was struggling on *The Real*, and for the first time in my life I told someone about the letter that had planted those nasty seeds of Ugly and Goofy in my head so many years ago. I got the words out, and before I could grab our server for another mimosa, Andrea was setting me straight.

"Tamera, I am so sorry that happened to you. But I have to tell you that no one defines who you are but you. Do not listen to this insecurity living inside you. Do not ever agree to being someone you aren't. You are not ugly or goofy. You cannot let these mean comments you are getting from viewers on the show challenge who you know you are."

She took a light sip of her mimosa for effect, gently curled her lips, and sank back into perfect lighting while I let her words sink in.

I knew she was right, I was letting my insecurity ring louder than my truth. That insecurity from my childhood was managing to whisper negative messages into my adulthood. It took a while for me to fully shed Ugly and Goofy from my life once and for all. I loved her for what she said. I just hoped that the pain of the words from that letter, sent so many years before, would eventually fade away, never leaving a scar.

cele

The Sunday episodes came and went over the course of those seven years when I was on *The Real.* I knew how blessed I was to have my job, and it got easier for me to speak up on the show, but leaving my husband and young children every week still hurt my heart. And while Andrea had helped me finally kick Ugly and Goofy to the curb, it was harder to ignore the darkness that is the free rein people have on social media to slay your character. It helped that I wasn't alone. The women of *The Real* are all like sisters to me, and they provided the positivity that kept me going. I loved sharing our thoughts and feelings about everything from fashion and beauty to current events, but the negativity from the outside world could be triggering. The negative comments about everything from my views on taking control of my sexuality to my choice of husband were picked apart. Being a talk show host is almost like being a fancy piñata. Piñatas are colorful, pretty, and clearly meant to entertain, but then all of a sudden people are lining up to beat that pretty thing repeatedly with sticks until all of its insides spill out onto the floor. But that's not all, folks! Then there's a stampede to grab onto every little thing that came out of it. Your insides are being greedily eaten while you lie there utterly destroyed, waiting for someone to sweep what's left of you into the trash.

I know this is a hard concept to understand. Try to imagine if every day after you got home from work *anyone* got to comment on every little aspect of your job performance! I envision something like this:

Hi, Mary:

It's Pam from HR!

We understand you had a conversation today with your colleagues regarding the upcoming holiday party.

Apparently since EVERYONE brought cupcakes last year you suggested a "sign-up sheet" would be a good idea so everyone knows what others are bringing.

WHO DO YOU THINK YOU ARE EXACTLY? Who are you to decide there should be a VARIETY of foods at a party? IS AN ALL-CUPCAKE PARTY NOT GOOD ENOUGH FOR YOU? You really are unbelievably uppity! You really aren't who I thought you were! THIS IS VERY DISAPPOINTING.

And just when you're thinking, *Fine, that's the last time I try to help out with the holiday party*, you get this.

Hi, Mary!

Happy Monday, Pam from HR again.

It's been brought to our attention that you've been asking colleagues if they'd "like a cup of coffee" and then you've been taking it upon yourself to procure them their caffeinated beverage of choice. What exactly are you trying to do? What are you saying? That your colleagues don't have enough energy? That they lack pep and vigor? And how do you think Jim feels? Are you judging him for having bags under his eyes? How rude of you to point out his fatigued complexion to the entire company by offering to purchase him a coffee! This behavior is outrageous and will not be tolerated.

Have a great afternoon, and I'll be in touch tomorrow to chastise you for more benign behavior that will either be viewed as totally offensive or taken out of context!

Can you trust me when I tell you it's not easy to describe what this level of scrutiny felt like? Other than I couldn't win.

After tapings I'd retreat into my dressing room. I had created a shabby-chic haven of warm neutrals and clean white lines. I'd sit on my overstuffed sofa, kick off my heels, and close my eyes—willing the stress of the day to evaporate off me. Never underestimate the healing power of a well-decorated room.

As a woman, it's easy to believe you have to be everything for everyone: wife, mother, breadwinner, teacher, chef, therapist, hair stylist, interior decorator, magician, plumber, event planner, chauffer, travel agent, librarian, sock finder, role model, lifeguard, spokesperson, entertainer. It's a never-ending to-do list for all women—and I was giving my all on TV every day, and still ending up on someone's list of WOMEN WHO HAVE DONE WRONG. It was time to let go and start doing more for me so I could just do my job. I was devoting all my energy toward staying happy and working overtime to keep the negativity at bay. If I wanted there to be anything left of me, something was going to have to change.

So one day after taping, I lit my dressing room candle and told myself to breathe. I opened my eyes and looked at the beautiful black-and-white photographs of my family that

I had hung on the wall of my dressing room. The woman in the picture wasn't a teenage TV star anymore. She was grown up and wise enough to recognize that the fear she felt was an echo of something that had happened a long time ago. I thought about what Andrea said to me, and her words felt like a balm to my heart. I had to stop giving so much power to people who knew nothing about me. Moving forward, I carried my friend's wise words like a good luck charm—I pledged that I would never allow anyone else to tell me who I am. And if someone decides I don't meet their expectations of who I should be? I do not have to agree with them. Reminding myself of this regularly was the only way I was going get through the next few years, and this delightful little nugget of wisdom helped me feel stronger each day.

TAMERAISM
Only you can define who you are.

Something changes when we realize we are the authors of our own stories, because others are constantly trying to edit us aren't they? People like to gloss over our rough bits until our story is smooth enough for their liking. Only you get to decide what to do with the complexities and nuances of your story. Whether it's Pam from HR, your in-laws (sorry, no one has better in laws than I do), your neighbor, your ex—the story they've told themselves about you is their own. Only you can know the truth and you have approval over the final draft! You are under no obligation to agree with their assessment of your cooking, your career, your mothering, your hopes, and dreams. Only you get to set the parameters of your story. And if it helps, take a minute right and just get to the core of your story. I can tell you it's not easy to recover from being ripped apart like a birthday piñata, and Ugly and Goofy had me convinced for a long time that my story wasn't all mine to tell. I know differently now, and had I understood that I had the power to tell Ugly and Goofy what to do with themselves, I would have written them off a long time ago and celebrated their demise by devouring a scrumptious little raspberry-lemon-tart.

Dear Person Who Said I Was Ugly and Goofy,

I do not agree with your assessment of me! But because I know who I am (a generous, warm, loving and forgiving woman) if you were ever to sit at my table, I'd hand you a cookie, throw a smile your way and agree to put it all behind us. I forgive you because there is just too much sweetness in life to be had, and I intend to enjoy every precious drop of it.

CHAPTER TEN

Drama and Dressing Rooms

Imagine me, four long years into my contract at *The Real* with another three to go, crying in my dressing room. My eyes are already puffy, and it's going to be hard to cover this up with makeup. I feel lost and overwhelmed and cannot imagine getting through the week, much less the rest of my contract.

As hard as I tried to stay positive, and as much as I adored my coworkers, I still felt trapped. It was one of the unhappiest times of my life. I suffered horrible anxiety, I'd throw up in my dressing room, I drank way too much, and every single day I was confronted with a fresh new version of hellish histrionics.

If you're thinking, *Boo-hoo, Tamera didn't like her fancy talk show job. I'm over this. I'm putting this book in the donation pile right now*, just hang on a second! I pride myself on being a positive person. There isn't a silver lining that I can't find. Give me a big glass of lemon juice and I will not stop until I find enough sugar to transform that sour nastiness into something delicious. So, before we get into my personal struggle, know that the sweetness in my glass came from the people I worked with at *The Real*. The women who sat with me at that table were brilliant, creative, interesting, funny, passionate, beautiful, and exuberant! I love those women! *Love*. Let's go ahead and garnish that glass of lemonade with a nice big sprig of fresh mint. My job on *The Real* resulted in my cohosts and me winning the Daytime Emmy Award for best hosts! You know who else won an Emmy in that same category? *Oprah Winfrey, that's who*. Also Kelly Ripa and Ellen DeGeneres. That's good company! This is something all of us from *The Real* did together, and I'm very proud of it! A round of lemonade for everyone!

On the outside, it probably looked like I had everything, and on many levels this was true. I had crossed some pretty big items off on the grand checklist of life. I had my family, a wonderful husband, two kids, a really good-paying job, and my health. Check, check, and check! But inside was where you'd fine the sour side of things. I felt pulled apart, worn down, on edge, full of dread, anxious, and scared. I felt like I was walking on a never-ending supply of ultradelicate eggshells. Then I'd open my mouth, and just like that, *crack*, and I'd find myself standing in another huge, sticky, and sometimes humiliating mess. The backlash always hurt, but things got much worse for me when my husband was dragged into the mix.

In Texas, I certainly experienced racism but shortly after we had made the official move to California, I had a racist encounter that rocked me to my core. I was getting used to my new school and was starting to make some friends. I played with a little girl I'll call Jessica. (It was the '80s. You couldn't throw a stone without hitting a girl named Jessica.) This Jessica was a rambunctious little girl with long blonde braids and a hearty laugh. We'd run around the playground together, never short on that supply of extra potent kid energy. We'd play hopscotch and see who could go higher on the swings—I'm talking about classic after-school playing.

"Tamera! Let's go! We've got to be somewhere."

I heard my mom's voice calling me while I was midair on the swing. I stopped pumping my legs, and when I slowed down enough, I jumped off.

"Jessica, I gotta go. That's my mom."

Jessica hopped off her swing and walked with me to where my mom was waiting . . . The rapid tapping of my mom's foot was code for *Tamera, please get a move on it because I do not want to sit in rush hour traffic.* When Jessica saw my mother, she looked like she had seen a ghost.

"Wait, *that's* your mom?"

I didn't understand why Jessica looked so surprised. My mother is on the short side, but I didn't think it was anything to freak out about. Jessica kept staring at my mom like she was from outer space. She waved goodbye, and I climbed in the back seat of the car to do my homework en route to another audition.

The next day, I approached Jessica at recess. She was hanging on the monkey bars with a few other kids, and she didn't look happy to see me. But I didn't move, because I thought for sure she'd want to play. I started to think I must have done something wrong. After an awkward minute, Jessica realized I wasn't going away. She jumped off the monkey bars to talk to me.

"I can't play with you anymore, Tamera."

I barely registered what she was saying. We had been hanging out together for weeks! It didn't make any sense. What did I do?

"I can't be your friend because your mom is Black."

After spewing those hateful words at me, Jessica turned around and ran off to the slide with the other kids. I just stood there by myself, my heart beating hard, my hands shaking. This wouldn't be the last time I experienced racism, but it was the first time I saw how painfully cruel humans can be to one another. I was numb, angry, shocked—and confused. As tears started to stream down my face I thought, *How could someone who I thought liked me actually hate me? How can skin color matter like this?* The blatant meanness of the situation overwhelmed me, and I actually felt sick.

So when viewers started posting hideous comments about my husband while I was on *The Real*, my feelings were intense. I was a grown woman with many successes and a bunch of life experiences under her belt! But launch a few nasty comments my way about my husband, and I'm not going to sit back and take it. It's shocking to me how casually people inflict cruelty on each other. While I did brush off plenty of negativity, the assumptions made about my husband were not something I could stay quiet about. I mean, would you? Apparently, some viewers objected to the fact that I married a white man. Some viewers took it a few steps further, taking things out of context and creating a false narrative and called my husband a racist. This one was a real puzzle. My husband is not a racist. Perhaps it's because he worked for Fox News? My husband was not a talking head, he wasn't an opinion host spewing any sort of negativity on Fox. He was a hard news correspondent. A badass reporting from warzones, floods, hurricanes, tornadoes, mass shootings, earthquakes—*the hard stuff*. This line of commentary went on for so long and hurt enough (and social media has made it ever so easy for people to get directly in touch with me) that I had to put an end to it. So one day, I looked right into the camera on national television and said for once and for all, "My husband is not a racist." On some level I couldn't believe that I actually had to do this. I had risen to the top of my industry, but I still had to defend my choice of husband? I'm not going to lie: that hurt me.

The weird speculation about my marriage didn't stop there. As we've been in the journey that is this book for a while now, you've gathered that I am a self-proclaimed girly girl with a strong domestic side—I love to cook and bake, and I thoroughly enjoy creating a home for my family. I live to decorate! And I understand that this may sound strange (I really do), but I love to clean. When I return home from a project, after greeting my family with hugs and kisses I go right for the broom, and I don't play. Floors, countertops, the stove, the backsplash—all of that is no match for me. When I'm satisfied with the state of things, I grab a bag of lemons from my freshly wiped-down and organized refrigerator. Once I've artfully arranged those lemons in a gorgeous bowl for the island, my work is done. I have successfully reclaimed my space. Is there something so wrong with taking pride in my own home that I helped earn the money to pay for? I wouldn't have thought so, but somehow this resulted in a series of comments with the twisted theme of *Tamera is a 1950's housewife and her husband controls her!* Hello? Just because I know I clean better than Adam (or honest to God, better than 99 percent of humanity) doesn't mean I'm living like some throwback of a wife. I *earn*, and I clean. It's that simple.

As you know by now, I am a Christian woman, and I didn't think this side of me would come under fire, but it did. I am failing to remember the specific subject of this particular episode of *The Real*, but the gist was marriage and relationships. When I said, "You have to die for yourself each day," the reaction was so intense you would have thought I had said, "The world is flat, the sun revolves around the earth, and unicorns are real." My comment was interpreted as something along the lines of "Sacrifice everything about yourself for your husband because you are a vessel of service for your man!!!" Sigh. For realz? I'm not a theologian, but I believe the Bible talks about "die for self" in some form or another about twenty-five times (I looked it up). And we all should! Because what it really means is this:

Although I'd love to spend the next two hours in this bathtub soaking and sipping this wonderful Pinot Noir in my seaweed collagen face mask, my partner really does need my support tonight at his company holiday party—so

I *will* wipe this stuff off my face, haul myself out of here, and get dressed.

Is this such a hard concept to understand? That we don't get to do whatever we want all the time when we are in a relationship? Adam might be out having a grand time riding his motorcycle with his friends, but he'll say good-bye to all that fun when it's time to come home and get fancied up for a red-carpet event he'll be attending with me. We're a team, and it's give and take. Now that I've made myself clear (I hope, anyway), can we agree that we do indeed "die for self" a little tiny bit every day for the people we love? If you want to enjoy life on this planet (and yes, I know it's round), with or without a partner, prepare to make an occasional sacrifice or compromise! I'd like to be soaking in a tub right now! But I've got work to do and kids to feed.

TAMERAISM
Things happen for you, not to you.

I think it all boils down to this: when I was on *The Real* I didn't feel like I had control over my own narrative. Comments were so easily manipulated, and people were so hungry to criticize. While I know I was blessed on many levels to have that job, it is highly disruptive to feel like strangers are creating a storyline for the life you live when you go home at night. Ladies, it was painful. I felt like I needed mental boxing gloves every time I went to work. I didn't think I could make it through to the end of my commitment. I legit worried I was headed for a real breakdown. Now *that* would have given people something to talk about. But in the end *The Real* gave me another gift. I came to the conclusion that this was happening for me and not too me. I had a choice. I could be like a diamond and shine as a result of the pressure, or I could remain a dark, sad, and worthless lump. *Which would it be, Tamera?* At that moment I dipped into an inner strength I didn't know I had. I moved forward, I kept talking (and I still upset people), but I didn't back away. I kept my focus on being a positive and authentic voice, and I started to actually see the positive impact I was having. To the woman on the street who said, "You talked so openly about postpartum depression—I don't know if I would have made it out alive if I hadn't heard that," it is you who saved me. To all the women who sent a kind word my way, you were my purpose. You were the reason I showed up every morning.

You showed me that I made a difference and that the human spirit can triumph during challenging times. I thank you for this from the bottom of my heart. I eventually decided to leave *The Real*. I packed up my shabby-chic dressing room, and I carefully put my family photographs in boxes. I loaded up all my extra shoes and gathered up my favorite coffee cup. But the best thing I took with me, the greatest parting gift I have ever received, was knowing I made an impact. And can we talk about making an impact for a quick minute? Because it is so very easy to brush off the impact we make as women. Every simple thing we do from the moment we get up until our very tired head hits the pillow at night makes an impact. You don't have to be splitting the atom or saving endangered species to make a real impact. Helping a little child brush her teeth, buttering your beloved's toast, putting on a fresh pot of coffee, helping with homework, driving to school, laughing with a colleague, chatting with a friend, calling your mother, running an errand for a neighbor, walking the dog, packing lunches, making dinner . . . the list of things that women do to make a positive mark on someone else's life could fill volumes of books. You have the power to make a difference every single day—and you do. And please know that I see you. And while we won't always be able to sit here like we are now, with our sweet treats and glasses of wine, please remember that I'm in awe of everything that you do. We are all our own number one encouragers, and that takes strength. So be kind to yourself, because your world is depending on you.

CHAPTER ELEVEN

Closets and Cars

You'll notice the mommy guilt in my voice first. It's like you can actually hear that my energy is low. I speak quieter, like I'm a slightly muted version of myself, exhausted by the constant push and pull of everything, and I'm worried I'm not giving my kids enough of me. But let me quickly address something before we get into this conversation. You might be thinking, *Well, blah, blah, blah, Tamera! You're an actress, you probably have six nannies, a driver, a chef, a masseuse, and a masseuse for your dog. What do you have to complain about?* First, I don't have a nanny, and that's by choice (notable exception: I had a nanny when the kids were babies, and I was commuting to Los Angeles). Adam and I feel that our parents raised us, and we want to raise our kids. It's not perfect, but between myself and their very hands-on dad we manage. I know I am blessed, and I am aware of my good fortune, but I don't have a chef/masseuse/dog masseuse . . . *I'm not Oprah.**

But there is something all women have in common regardless of income or status, and that's the fact that there are only twenty-four hours in a day. During those twenty-four hours mothers need to perform an extraordinary number of things (and you need to be asleep during a good portion of those hours to function normally)! It's no easy feat to care for the important needs of others while holding yourself together—it's hard enough to find the time to shower, eat breakfast, get a glass of water, pray, and just breathe. Then there's the great big list of questions parents always have floating around in their heads. It's never ending, right? *Who is driving—or are you picking up? Where is the game, and are we in charge of bringing the snack? Is the baseball uniform washed? When is the science project due? We have to leave for gymnastics in five minutes! Where is Ariah's leotard? Keys. Where are my keys? There is no school on Friday? Seriously? Are you sure? Did you pick up coffee on the way home? Because we can't NOT have coffee! Did we buy a birthday gift for the party? STOP! Turn the car around right now because we forgot the gift!*

---

*I have no idea whether or not Oprah has a masseuse and/or a dog masseuse. I'm simply referring to Oprah as the pinnacle of achievement.

The complications of motherhood are beautiful and precious, and I'm grateful for it all, but let's be honest, it's also really hard to navigate at times. So if you've ever nearly lost your mind because you couldn't find your son's left shoe, please know I get you (P.S. Check in the laundry basket). I also will not judge you if your kids' socks do not match. Priorities!

I am not the first woman to combine kids and work. Nor am I the first woman to say that being a mother and working full time is an enormous challenge. I will say this, though—I'm not conflicted about it. Not at all. I love my work as passionately as I love my family, and my kids are being raised by a woman who is living out her dream. Acting is woven into the fiber of my very being. If you were to pull that part of me out, I wouldn't be my best self, and that's who I want to be for them . . . my best self. Acting gives me purpose, making movies thrills me, and I'm fueled by the challenge. When I'm not filming, I feel excited just thinking about what opportunity could come along next. It could be anything, I could play a CEO of a huge international company, a zookeeper, or a teacher. *Who knows?* Acting keeps me on my toes, and I like that. On a more basic level . . . Acting also pays the bills. As for the flip side of this coin, being a mother is a joy beyond anything I've ever experienced. The deep level of love is astonishing, right? There's no other way to describe it. Those two tiny people have cracked my heart and soul wide open. Being Aden and Ariah's mother is the privilege of a lifetime. *So if you're not conflicted about it, why all the fuss, Tamera?* Stick with me. I'm getting there.

I am a proud working mother, but right now, this very second, I happen to be working from the inside of my closet. Allow me to share the view: The bottom shelf holds all of my casual "mom shoes"—sneakers for working out, a brightly colored pair of Converses, the Vans I thought would be convenient because I could just slip them on but that turned out to be way too skater girl for me. Slightly to the left and directly at eye level are the hunter boots. They're so sturdy they practically stand at attention, like they're proud to be khaki green. In my head these boots transport me from Napa directly to a moor in the English countryside. Then there's the sandals, lots of them— strappy, high heeled, and the ones that are still cute but comfy enough to walk in. Now I'm looking up toward the top shelf where the super-sexy high heels live. The date night shoes. Louboutins with the signature red bottoms, shiny gold Manolos, and the badass Valentino Rockstuds. Clothing is arranged by type and season, flowy summer dresses here, long-sleeve dresses next, and wow, it's been ages since I wore that grey number—it might be time to edit. *Thanks for the impromptu tour of your closet, Tam, but what's the point? Why are we in here?* Right! I'm in here, ensconced among all the shoes and clothes because it is nearly impossible to get anything done with little people around, and *that* is what the fuss is all about.

I've taken business calls in this very closet with my kids pounding on the door. I've driven home and sat in my car in my own driveway because I needed just a few more minutes to finish writing an email, and I knew it would be impossible to do once I walked in the front door. I've done phone interviews from my bathroom (which you would think would offer a woman some privacy, but we all know that's not necessarily true). It's when I hear those little voices asking for me, those adorable tiny hands knocking on the closet door when I know full well that I could be leaving for several weeks in the near future to work, that the guilt hits me like a slap in the face. And oh, does it sting!

I am not about to wow you with a perfect solution to the mommy guilt woes. (An occasional glass of a fine Cabernet is about as close as you can get to that fictional perfection.) I'm not going to pretend that I can solve the childcare crisis in this country (and I believe me, I know I am incredibly fortunate that I can pay for help when I need to). There are no magic words to fix those *I just need five minutes to take this call, and I can hear that you need me to get you a cookie/*

find your baseball/blow your nose/answer your question about why the stars don't fall from the sky. But you gotta wait a minute! moments. Working moms of the world, you know exactly what I mean, right? We all know our children will not become serial bank robbers if we don't drop everything and get them a cookie the second they want one—but that doesn't stop your heart from feeling that twinge. You want to be there (and you often *are* there), but your attention is divided sometimes, because you are doing it all.*

When I'm in this closet, about to fall into a sloppy, crying mess (I really should keep a box of tissues in here, and some snacks, actually), I pick myself up, get out of the closet, and look in the mirror to remind myself, *You are your number one encourager—you've got this.* This isn't about not having emotional support—I have a supportive partner, friends, family! This is about tapping into that part of your soul that truly knows you are capable of hard things. I'm talking about having rock-solid faith in your abilities to nail your career and be a loving, devoted parent. I learned very quickly that if I wanted to survive in Hollywood, I'd have to be my number one encourager. Because you know what feels amazing? Nailing an audition, truly *killing it.* I'd put this feeling on par with some of life's other big-ticket

---

*I'm not dissing anyone's partners here. Working and being a parent is a lot no matter what.

moments—the last final exam of your college career, discovering that dress you've been eyeing is on sale, the sip of a crisp rosé on the first day of summer. It's joyful. What does not feel amazing is getting the *we've decided to go in a different direction* call. What? Were we in the same room? Because I thought I did great! Ego deflated like a popped balloon. When I was a kid, after a number of great auditions that resulted in no jobs and yet another big fat pity party for myself, my no-nonsense mother was done.

"Tamera, enough of this. You need to be your number one encourager! Sure, I can tell you you're talented. You can listen to the casting director or your agent, but regardless of the feedback, you need to believe in your abilities deep down in your core. You need to stay grounded, believe in yourself. The world is full of yessers and naysayers, so no matter what, you need to be the number one person encouraging yourself."

Why are mothers always right?

I've stopped focusing on what I can't control . . . why a casting director didn't pick me, why a show I was going to host didn't get picked up, how the Elsa cake I ordered for my daughter's birthday ended up saying "Happy Birthday, Angela!" Life is full of crazy mishaps and big disappointments, but I've stopped blaming them on myself. I've stopped believing they will define my life or my kids' lives. I'm my number one encourager!

Give me a second so I can crawl out of this closet, wipe away my tears, and look at myself in the mirror and say, "You are doing a great job." Now that I'm out of the closet, and we're clear on why we must encourage ourselves, let me share a few other ideas that have helped me keep it together when it feels like it could all fall apart. I like to think of these ideas as mommy guilt first aid.

BAND-AID #1: YOU HAVE EIGHTEEN SUMMERS. DO SOME SERIOUS MEMORY MAKING.

By making summer extra special in the little ways, you are creating lifelong memories, as well as opportunities for you to be present and witness your excellent mothering firsthand. You are a joy spreader.

Time can get really whacky when you become a parent. If a baby keeps you up crying for two hours at night, it feels like a decade (and you will likely age during the course of that single night). That toddler who just outgrew his shoes five minutes ago? Suddenly he's applying for medical school. In motherhood the days can be long, but the years are very, very short. That's why you've got to treat your summers like the rare and precious jewels they are. I assure you there is no need to resign from your job. But there are *only* eighteen summers between the time your children arrive on this earth and they become full-fledged adults with their own busy lives to live. *Use them.* No elaborate European vacations are required, just some good old-fashioned summer fun. Summer is about family car trips, carnivals, the zoo, and lemonade stands. I will have done my job right if our kids remember our epic summer barbecues. Friends in the pool, yacht rock on the sound system. Adam flipping burgers in his TAMERA'S KITCHEN BUT I'M THE COOK apron. We'll have rosé chilling and margaritas to start—then move on to light reds and Chardonnays. There's food, drinks, laughter, wrinkled toes from hours in the water—and falling asleep absolutely exhausted from the fun of it all. The simplest of summer activities make for the best memories.

BAND-AID #2: THE BUSY KID APPROACH TO PARENTING

This one is simple. If you keep your kids busy they don't have time to be unhappy about anything, and that's a huge win for busy moms.

As far as Adam and I are concerned, our kids can be astronauts, accountants, veterinarians, athletes, actors, or chefs. The profession itself isn't what's important here. It's the passion that's key. Passion = Loving Your Work = Loving Your Life. To help foster a passion in our kids we keep them busy doing all sort of things at all times. Aden plays baseball and soccer. (Adam is the coach!) He adores baseball so much that he gets up on his own, gets dressed in his uniform, and wakes *us up*. Now if I can just train him to wake us up by bringing us coffee. Ariah loves gymnastics. They're both very, very curious about acting (we'll see about that), they've done STEM camp, and they've done a program where they hang out on a farm and take care of animals and tend the land. I'm open to just about any activity, as long as they're doing something. The busy kid approach to parenting has several benefits. Busy kids don't have time to get in trouble. Busy kids get fresh air and exercise, and they connect with other kids. And most important, I believe that if my kids feel that spark, whether it's for baseball, acting, or cooking, they'll develop an understanding of why my work is important to me. I'm not just running off to shoot movies—I'm modeling what it looks like to be madly in love with your family and your job.

BAND-AID #3: JUST BAKE SOMETHING.

This one never fails. If I pull out baking ingredients and the stand mixer, tiny feet come running my way, all smiles and shouting, "Mommy, what are you baking?" You can transform yourself into a

*maternal domestic goddess by making a treasured family recipe or
just ripping open a box of brownie mix.*

Never underestimate the power of a good homemade
cookie. Bake with your kids. Let them measure ingredients
and toss flour around. I'm a cleanliness freak, but I pur-
posely pause the part of myself that would scream, "Did
she really just drop a raw egg on my clean floor?" Don't
worry about getting fancy when you bake, and know that if
you choose to go the Duncan Hines route your secret is safe
with me. My early baking memories with my mom involve
standing together at the counter, stirring batter for a lemon
cake from a mix. We added our own personal flair by dec-
orating the top with fresh strawberries. I have yet to taste
a more delicious cake. Experiment if you want, and bake
every chocolate chip cookie recipe you can find. Try out
an old family favorite. It doesn't matter what you bake or
if your cake looks like the losing creation on an episode of
Nailed It! It's the time together that matters. There's nothing better than gathering around a table with your family
to eat something that was mixed together with love.

TAMERAISM

You have to be your number one encourager.

I am out of my closet (for now at least) sitting at the island in my kitchen, everything neat and in its place. Soon the kids will run in the door with their backpacks, home from school and hungry for a prehomework snack. Today I'm here, and I'll give them each a cookie and ask them about their day. I'll listen to stories about recess and what they learned in science class. I'll get them going on their homework, and I'll get dinner started. As I start to slice veggies while my kids are working on math worksheets, I think about what it will be like in two weeks when I fly to the other side of the country to shoot a movie. The early morning rush to get ready for school will be replaced by an ultra-ultra-early arrival on set, followed by a long day of shooting. I'll be engaged in my work, but I'll miss everything about them—their smiles, their smell, their laughter, and their hugs. But when the mommy guilt starts to sneak in, I'll lean on my number one encourager . . . *me*. I'll remind her that she's doing her best, she's living her dream, and she's setting an example for her children. I'll also remind her that this job will end soon, and she'll be home before she knows it, back in the kitchen making more cookies. There'll be flour all over the counter, but that's just fine. Because who knows when she'll have to leave again? For now, never mind the mess—we'll just bake.

CHAPTER TWELVE

Turquoise Now and Forever

On the night of November 7, 2018, not too long after going to sleep, my husband's phone rang. It was Arik, Adam's brother, "Alaina went out dancing with friends, and there was a shooting—it's all I know right now." A shooting? Alaina? *This is impossible, she has to be okay.* The same nightmare that has destroyed too many families in this country had arrived in our bedroom—and unfortunately the nightmare was real.

Alaina Housley. My sweet, sweet Alaina, you stole my heart when you were just five years old. By now you all know (I'm talking to you, readers!) I was emailing back and forth with Adam before I met him in person. In the first picture he sent me he was standing next to a tiny, bright-eyed, mocha-skinned beauty whose smile was larger than life. Alaina . . . your uncle was wise to include you in the first photo he shared with me, because who could resist your cuteness? Who wouldn't want to go out with a man who so clearly adored his niece? I'll admit it, when I first saw that picture, I thought, *Okay, I can definitely have kids with this man. If there's any chance they'll look like her, I'm all in!*

Alaina, you and I clicked instantly. We bonded over fun, girly things like manicures, hair braiding, makeup, and clothes. I was in love with Adam, and I was smitten with your entire family, but it didn't take me long to come to a surprising conclusion. That you, Alaina, were my favorite Housley. You know that, right, Alaina? And I'm sorry for Adam! But it's the honest-to-God truth. We sang so well together, too. I treasure the photograph of us right after we sang the national anthem together before the first Napa Valley 1839 soccer game. I often show that picture to people because it captures the essence of our relationship. Our faces show lots of love with a big side of silly. We look so proud and happy in that picture! Remember how hard it is to hit that crazy high note at the end? That note is no joke! That day you taught me that there is something even more joyful than singing, and that's singing with someone whom you love with all your heart.

In true Housley-Mowry fashion, you chose to matriculate at Pepperdine. You followed in the footsteps of both of your parents, of your Uncle Adam, me, and of course Tia. A bright, outgoing girl—you probably could have studied anywhere you wanted to, but you were proud to step into a family tradition. I don't know how, but you managed to teach yourself to play the ukulele. I remember how you blew everyone's mind at the school talent show. Adam filled me in on your brilliant performance in *Les Miserables*. I was out of town and so sad to miss your performance, to miss seeing you in your element. You loved *Hamilton* as much as I did. Werk! And I was thrilled that you were theatre-curious, falling in love with acting and auditioning for plays in college. You knew I had your back—whatever you needed, advice, support, a last-minute mani-pedi. But this is the part that haunts me sometimes. Alaina, you wanted me to come see you to talk about acting and your new life in college, and I couldn't make it work. I didn't think much of it, because I was going to see you at Aden's birthday party the next week. In a million years I couldn't have imagined I'd never see you again. It's impossible to make sense of this. Someone with a gun went into a bar and stole your life along with the lives of eleven other innocent people. I ache for everything that was stolen. Your graduation from Pepperdine, your first job after college, the traveling you would have done, the men you would have dated, helping you through your first broken heart, the songs you would have sung, your wedding (you stole the show in mine you looked so pretty!), your first baby. We were robbed of all your potential—your entire future.

Your uncle drove down to Thousand Oaks to try to find you. He had covered mass shootings before, and yet it was unthinkable that you could be involved in one. I called the emergency hotline so many times that I was gently and kindly told *they would call me* when there was information. Your iPhone said that you were in the bar where the shooting took place hours and hours after the event happened, and we knew what that probably meant. But the little thread of hope was not something that was easy for any of us to let go of. Finally, your dad got the word. "She's gone," he said to your uncle. Those two little words carried so much power. An unbelievable amount of grief—*She's gone.* It is not possible to describe what any of us felt. I can't tell you what it was like to tell Ariah and Aden that their cousin was gone. Honestly, Alaina, I'm not entirely sure the words to describe this level of pain actually exist.

The Napa police drove down to where you were. You were brought home with a police escort—and the cops were crying too. The worst thing I have ever seen in my life was your mother's face when you arrived in that long black car. Her baby had come home, and she crumpled.

She wailed. I don't know how she survived that moment, because this was not the way you were supposed to come home from college. Seeing you in that car was a horrible reminder that this nightmare was real, and it wasn't going to end. The cops escorted you—silently, but with lights on, to the cemetery. The outpouring of support and love from the people of Napa was incredible. They lined the streets for you and your family. You wouldn't think something like that could help, but it did. You were loved. Of all the people who saved me from constant despair, it was your mother. She should not have had to save me, but she did. As we were approaching the second anniversary of your death and the pain was still raw, she said, "Tamera, I've realized something. Alaina was never fully mine. She belonged to God. I might have given birth to her, but her mission here on earth is done. She's with Him now." What a brave and wise thing to say—what a generous way to move forward in life after experiencing such pain! That's your mom, Alaina. She's really something. I learned that day how much love can hurt. Losing you hurt so much, and it still hurts a lot, but losing you also taught me to love. Even harder. I am going to love my people at full capacity—because we have no idea what's going to happen, Alaina. You're not even here, but you still taught me to love deeper, more fully, and without any reservation at all. I'm spreading as much love as I can around this world, and it's all thanks to the privilege of knowing you.

cele

Alaina loved watching Hallmark movies with her grandmother Judy. Alaina would be comfy in her leggings and a hoodie, curled up on the couch with a blanket while eating giant bowls of popcorn. Judy would be perched her in favorite chair with a big smile on her face. When Christmas rolled around and the supply of holiday-themed movies was never ending, Christmas cookies were added to the snack menu. I remembered that Alaina had once asked me, "Aunt Tam, how come you aren't in Hallmark movies?" I think my response might have been along the lines of "Well, I wish!" I was still on *The Real* at the time, and I was struggling there. I missed acting so much—but I had no idea if movies would ever be in the cards for me again. It had been seven years since I had done any acting at all, and my first Hallmark meeting hadn't gone well. I loved Hallmark movies as much as Alaina and Judy did, and I always felt I'd fit right in there. I mean, c'mon, right?! A huge roster of sweet, funny, and highly entertaining movies? Sign me up, please! Who am I kidding? Back then, "Please, please,

please, please sign me up" ran through my head on repeat. It was something I really wanted.

I was so thrilled to have my first meeting with Hallmark that you would have thought I was a little kid who had been set free in a toy store with an unlimited budget. I was sitting down with the executive team to talk about potentially starring in and producing some movies. The meeting was *meh*. It was the meeting equivalent of a kindly form letter: "We are all such big fans of your work... We all loved *Sister, Sister*... You were great in *Twitches*... It's been fun to watch you grow up... What are you doing next?" I was beyond thrilled by the idea of joining Hallmark, but I sensed that excitement was not being mirrored back to me. And I was right. I soon received the meeting equivalent of *it's not you it's me* in the form of *We don't have anything for you right now*. Big sigh. I know, I know, it's not something that can be taken personally. It's part of the process, blah, blah, blah. Can I just say that sometimes the process is a real bummer? But the idea of Alaina and Judy getting to see me on the Hallmark channel made my heart want to burst! That particular no was hard to take, because ultimately it meant a missed opportunity to make Alaina happy.

You know what's funny? I've been a devout Christian my entire life, but up to that point I hadn't spent much time pondering what happens in the afterlife. But Alaina changed that for me. I know this might sound crazy to some people, and I own that . . . but the lights in the house would flicker gently whenever I talked about my niece. Feeling her energy is like stumbling upon rare treasure.

Oh, also as you know by now, Tamera + flying (especially on a small plane) = a hot, anxious mess.

Those tiny planes I took back and forth from Napa to Los Angeles *freaked me out.* Talking to Alaina got me through those flights. I'd put on my seatbelt and say, "Lay, Lay! You know I don't like this!" I'd take a breath, put on my headphones, and listen to "Oceans" by Hillsong because it was one of our favorites and it brought me some comfort. Before I knew it, the plane was landing, and I believe she was with me the entire flight.

About a year after losing her I realized I needed to go to therapy. The bitterness and anger were more than I could handle. I was afraid to leave the house, afraid what could happen out in public. I was in a dark place, and I fell into a pit of bitterness so deep I wasn't sure I'd be able to climb out of it. I was angry at God, too, and that was a terrible feeling. During my first session, the therapist asked me a question: "What did Alaina's death teach you? What gift did Alaina give you?" I was really taken back by this question. *What did it teach me? What gift did she give me? What do you mean? She died at eighteen!*

There isn't a gift. There's nothing positive to take from this. I'm angry and in so much pain. I couldn't believe that she asked me such an incredibly hurtful question—but something, and I don't know what, told me to stick with it. Therapy was a long and intense process, but it helped me. The pain will never go away—but eventually I managed to climb out of that dark hole. I feel like I can breathe again. I still cry, though.

TAMERAISM
Live your life the way you want it to be starting right now.

Eventually that therapist revisited that same question: What gift did she give you? This time I knew the answer, and it was so very simple—the answer was *now*. Life your life now. Don't be afraid, don't wait for "the right" moment, don't hold back. Live. Life. Now. There's nothing to wait for! It might sound corny (and you know I'm not opposed to being a bit corny), but there is no dress rehearsal for life! This is it. Alaina taught me that. She taught me to live bigger. We all have different numbers. Some of us get eighty years, or more! Like my grandmother Cloretha who died at the age of eighty-nine, shortly after Alaina. I hope those two are together because they would make quite a team. Some people never make it out of the womb, and some get a few beautiful, precious years to grace this earth. Alaina's number was eighteen, and I'll never be okay with that—but she did teach me how to live. And I promise I'll do right by her. I will hold her cousins longer, I will laugh harder, I will be more patient, I will be bolder, I will sing more, and I'll never stop baking cookies.

The Real was quite a drama—and my future didn't exactly look bright when my contract was up. I could have renewed it. Even though it was the hardest job I had ever had, staying there would have been the safe move. My team reminded me that they couldn't guarantee there'd be any other opportunities for me, and didn't I want to play it safe? Remember the *no* from Hallmark! We can't promise you'll get different responses from anyone else. But no, I wanted to aim big, and I wanted to do it *now*. What possible reason could I have for waiting to follow my dream? And I do not believe it's a coincidence that shortly after Alaina died Hallmark signed me for four movies. I like to think she is happy about this.

I shot *A Christmas Miracle* the following August (yes, it's weird shooting Christmas movies in the height of summer), and I was terrified. I was playing a single mother—could I be believable? Naturally there's a Christmas romance—would I be able to have on-screen chemistry with the male lead? It had been such a long time since I had been in front of a camera as an actress. What if I just didn't have it anymore? I was worried my comic timing would be nonexistent. I was worried I'd be terrible. I was so freaked out that I was going to mess up my opportunity to act again that I said out loud (I didn't care who heard), "Alaina! All right! I'm scared. I haven't acted in seven years. I'm alone, and I need to know you're with me. I know this is a selfish ask, but can you help me out here? I need two things—and then I know I can get through this. I want to see your favorite color. Show me some turquoise, please! And okay, you're the only Alaina I've ever met! I want to meet someone else named Alaina."

A desperate move by a desperate actress. I'm not sure what I was thinking, and I don't know what I expected. What I do know is that my jaw hit the floor when I walked out onto the set. Smack in the middle of the office where my character worked, was—drum roll please . . . a beautifully decked-out turquoise-and-silver Christmas tree. Turquoise! Alaina would have loved this tree! The turquoise was a unusual take on a Christmas color scheme, but it totally worked. But that's not all of it. Just a few days later I was in the makeup trailer when a woman I hadn't seen before walked in and stated, "Hi, I'm going to be helping the makeup team. My name is Alaina." *Are you serious?* I wished Alaina could have been there to see this poor woman's face. She must have thought I was completely bananas because I broke out into tears right then and there. This was not a delicate tear or two rolling down my cheek situation. This was a full-on sobfest—get this woman some smelling salts and a fainting couch! It took extra long to do my makeup that day because I was all red and puffy. I don't think I could have gotten through my first movie without Alaina—I owe it all to her.

Alaina, you loved turquoise. Turquoise clothes, fingernails, furniture, jewelry—anything that didn't move you thought should be turquoise. Turquoise represents everlasting love, and sometimes I wonder if she knew that. It makes so much sense. Turquoise has so many hues to it—it spans from a bright blue all the way to a Tibetan green. I see Alaina in some of the earth's most brilliant creations—the color of the most exotic oceans, the highest and brightest skies. And I've even seen her in the touch of turquoise that sparkles in her cousin Aden's eyes. It's been three years already, and it gives me some comfort to see her in the sky and in the water because it's a sign that my memory of her isn't fading. I've made a promise to myself that I'll never let that happen. I think of her all the time—when I'm listening to music, when I'm walking around Napa, when I paint my nails, when I watch a Hallmark movie, when I hug her cousins, when I spend time with her incredible parents and her loving brother. I ask myself all the time, Is my memory of her sharp? Is it fading? Know that it's not, because I won't let that happen. I will keep her alive in my head and in my heart. And she will forever be my favorite Housley.

Chapter Thirteen

Tea, Treats, and Wine Forever

Wow, how long have we been sitting here together? There's been lots of cookies and tiny cakes, cups of tea, glasses of wine, many tears, and so many big laughs. I've loved every minute of it, even the parts that were so difficult for me to talk about. I'm grateful to you for helping me get through all of that. I'm grateful to you for listening. And here we are, at the end. How does someone even begin to wrap up a book about their own life? Seriously, how? Because I'm at a loss, and I'm not sure I even want this to end! Shall we have one more glass? Let's go out to the patio—the sun will be setting soon, and it is a spectacular thing to see.

I never imagined I'd end up in Napa. Los Angeles, sure. Landing in LA felt right even when I was a wannabe tween actress with no clue about where my life would go. There was something about it. I could feel the possibility in Los Angeles from day one. But Napa is different. This is where I've realized a completely different kind of dream. It's where I've put down roots and started raising my family. Not too long ago Adam and I bought a property out here. It's 49 acres. Crazy, right? When Adam wanted to buy this land I thought, *For what? What are we possibly going to do with all of this space?* Imagine me looking at it and waving my hands wildly. Who needs this much land!? He just smiled and me and said, "I don't know. We'll build it up bit by bit. We'll start with a house, and then we'll slowly figure out what we want to do with it all."

Adam is so practical, I'm the one who lives in fantasyland. I'm already jumping ahead to designs, room layouts, appliances, kitchen cabinets, bathroom fixtures, window treatments, closets, landscaping, color palates, furniture—the list goes on and on. I think, *How will we ever get this done?* It's going to take *for-evah.* And once it's finally finished everything will be perfect! I can picture myself sitting on my nonexistent deck, staring at the home we've built together, knowing I've finally done it all! We can now proceed with living our dream life in our dream house! Look at this marvelous universe we've created for our family! And I'm excited about this house—the holidays we'll host, the dinners we'll make, the memories we'll create, the tears and laughter . . . all of it. Normally I'd be all over this project with lists and plans. Scheduling meetings, running full steam ahead—pushing, pushing to get it finished so we can really start living.

Here's the funny thing about committing your life to paper. You see literally in black and white how much joy you've had on your journey. You understand that those times you were just holding out for the next relationship, next job, next goal, next big thing . . . it wasn't about the end goal. Every step in between mattered. Those steps between are where some of your best memories are made. Now that I've written about "hopeful tween actress Tamera," just waiting for her life to unfold and her dream to come true, I'm flooded with bright spots of joy from that tender time. Going out for brunch with the family—a big Sunday treat when our father came to visit us when we first moved to Los Angeles. The simple comfort of sitting at a table with your people, the *excitement of the waffle station* with its unlimited supply of strawberries and whipped cream. Visiting the wax museum together, wondering if we will ever become "famous." Sleeping next to Tia on an air mattress, missing our old house, but filled with anticipation about what was possible for us in Los Angeles. Sharing a dream with my twin was the most special of gifts. Those were the moments between, and they were everything.

Adam is right—we don't have to know exactly what we're doing with our space, but isn't it fun to imagine how it all could go? I can look out on this empty land and envision the ideal little universe I want to create for my people, but after writing these pages I understand that this universe already exists in my heart. I want raucous holidays. An envy-inducing Christmas tree, a table laden with cookies I've baked with my family while wearing matching pajamas. I want dinners with friends and family on a long table that stretches out under the Napa sunset. There will be vintage tablecloths and napkins, jars of wildflowers, dishes of lovingly prepared foods being passed around on heirloom china dishes. And of course, perfect wine pairing with each course. I want to cuddle with my kids and watch movies. I want to laugh with my besties until we nearly wet ourselves. Part of me wants to stop everything and throw myself into the project that is building this dream of a house, but I see now that I don't have to wait. Sharing my story with you has taught me that *my life is already happening.*

Your life is unfolding before you this very instant—and it's either your dream life or it's not. That's the part that's up to you. So what's it going to be? Do you ever wake up and think, *I have so much to tackle today . . . work, laundry, getting the kids to soccer on time! There isn't enough time in the day! When will this get easier?* I get that feeling completely.

Can you just trust me here? If you write the book of your own life twenty years from now, the memory of a soccer game will stand out like a precious jewel. You'll be dazzled by the memories of clean, tiny uniforms, the pregame excitement, the big smiles after a win... that time when something as simple as a Popsicle had the power to soothe the sadness of a loss. You know how utterly maddening it is when you need to leave for the game in five minutes and you've searched high and low for that uniform? How it makes you want to scream, and then you spot it sticking out from under the couch? You will remember this someday and laugh, because it is the essence of your life.

Take it from a woman who has just written a memoir. We focus on the big events. The light bulb moments, the successes, the heartbreaks, the game-changing career developments, and the milestones... marriage, babies, and death. These are bricks and stones that make up the foundation of our lives, but it's the little things we do that make it *a life well lived*. I see now that there are so many moments where we need to stop and just look around. It's okay to marvel at your child's hands (even if they are always sticky). Let yourself get lost in your partner's eyes, even if you gaze into them and think, *Why on earth are you incapable of keeping track of your car keys?*

I want the love of my family. I want more acting! I have

goals. But wrapping things up here, you've helped me see how special *the granular* is. The rushed breakfast before school drop-off. The first crushes, the spilled milk, the lost uniform, the mismatched socks...the gift of the utterly ordinary. And I do hope we meet again. Who knows how old I'll be in my second memoir? Who knows what path I'll take next? What obstacles I'll conquer or good times I'll share? But one thing remains constant—you will always be welcome here. There will always be coffee, wine, and cookies, because they go well with countless kinds of stories, and just like you, I have a lot of living left to do.

Acknowledgments

Thank you, Paula B. Vitale, for helping make the words in my head come to life in a way that only you can. I needed someone I could trust, but most importantly have fun with. Because why not, when I'm exposing my soul to the world? Even though we had to talk about some uncomfortable moments in my life, you made me feel at peace from the beginning. You get me; you really do.

Thank you, Mom and Dad, for raising me with the understanding that a person's character is most important of all. Dad, you taught me that life is a journey and it's OK to take detours along the way as long as you are true to yourself. Mom, you showed me that God and my faith will never steer me wrong. *I will lift up mine eyes unto the hills, from whence cometh my help.* Always.

To Tahj, Tavior, and Tia—the best siblings I could ask for. Thanks for always having my back and making this life ever so fun. Our laughs and conversation are things I shall never forget. Each of you are an inspiration to me and this world. What a gift you are.

To the love of my life, Adam. You believe in me when I do not believe in myself. My partner, my best friend: I'm forever grateful to walk alongside you in life. I consider myself blessed to be able learn the many lessons and enjoy the amazing adventures of life with you. To know you is to love you.

To Aden and Ariah: You are my everything. You're the reason I look forward to each day, to have a front row seat to experience what amazing people you two are becoming. I know as a parent it is my duty to teach you, but you two teach me daily. For that I consider myself blessed.

Krishan Trotman, what can I say? I'm so appreciative. You made one of my dreams come true! I've always wanted to write a book. Not just for the sake of it, but to inspire, encourage, and share. Thank you for believing in me, my truth, and my life story. Thanks for inspiring me to be at peace with sharing the story I have always wanted to tell.